WITNESS AND WORK

Witness and Work

Brian Allenby

Terra Nova Publications

Published in Great Britain by
Terra Nova Publications Ltd
PO Box 2400, Bradford on Avon, Wiltshire BA15 2YN

Cover design by Gazelle Creative Productions Ltd.

ISBN 1 90194 928 1

Printed in Great Britain
by Bookmarque Ltd, Croydon

Contents

INTRODUCTION 7

1. THE JOURNEY BEGINS 15

2. SAFETY CHECKS BEFORE WE DEPART 35

3. LESSONS FROM A BOAT —BOLDNESS! 41

4. A VISIT TO THESSALONICA 53

5. REVIVAL BEGINS AT HOME 63

6. CLIMBING IN THE LAND OF SHALLOW GRAVES 79

7. KNOW YOUR ENEMY 93

8. PERSECUTION, OPPOSITION AND PEACE 103

9. LIVING HOPE 113

Introduction

We live in a world where Jesus Christ is the only real and true hope. I suppose it is not surprising that the world does not believe this, but it is a dire tragedy and a shameful fact that of the people who call themselves Christians, a high percentage only 'half–believe' —or call into question—the essential truths of God's revelation. We recognise that there is no way in which the Christian churches will ever formulate a statement of faith that all can accept. But those of us who passionately believe, with all our hearts and souls, in the divinity of our Lord Jesus Christ, in his redeeming and saving death and resurrection, must stand at the centre, to enable these truths to be witnessed to a perishing and needy world. Much of that world spends around forty per cent of its life at work!

The apathy of Christians has allowed a very dangerous situation to arise. Many people have stopped believing in the God and Father of Jesus Christ, but this vacuum means that people are more inclined to believe anything. Many of the world's business schools are teaching a form of 'spirituality' which they say is essential, but that spirituality does not embrace anything that we as Christians would recognise as spirituality. We see companies asking their staff to attend yoga sessions which, superficially, might appear to be a harmless activity, but which, it turns out, requires the participant to 'purge the mind' and recite meaningless mantras. In recent times, new recruits to companies and organisations have often been asked for their star signs before being employed. There is growing interest in the occult and New Age movement. All these things are extremely dangerous.

We need to be bear in mind that Satan and hell are real, and that those who reject Christ face a lost eternity. There is a tendency among many Christians to downplay the work of Satan and the eternal destiny of the unredeemed — hell. It is almost as if this place was now 'politically incorrect', together with the word 'sin' that causes the problem in the first place! We must remember that the word sin comes from a root that means 'to fall short', and that we all fall seriously short of God's expectations, and so need to remain in a position of humility, always ready to repent.

Gracia Burnham, a missionary, wrote of her experiences as a captive of the Abu Sayyaf in the Philippines. Sadly, her husband was shot dead in crossfire during the rescue attempt. In the book she recounts Martin's life prior to their captivity, and I was struck by her recollection of a time when, as a member of a college missionary prayer fellowship, he had participated in a dramatic presentation of mission through the ages, taking the part of William Carey. I quote:

As a young child, I learned the importance of putting my best effort into all that I did, and completing each task that I started —a discipline that was to pay off in my later years on the mission field....

From the beginning God gave me the desire to know exactly what His word said... As I continued my study and meditation on His Word, I could not help but be impressed with the fact that we, as believers were simply not doing all that God commanded.

When His Word says, 'Go ye' He means Go ye! And when He says, 'into all the world,' He means all the world. 'To preach the gospel to every creature' means exactly that. God means exactly what He says.

He has commanded us to 'go and make disciples of all nations.' The promise that follows is 'Lo, I am with you always.' Do any of us have the right to play leapfrog with the command and (only) hug to the promise?[1]

This book is primarily (but not exclusively) aimed at those Christians for whom 'the world' means, in large measure, their workplaces. The Great Commission applies just as much in these settings as in other places of Christian mission.

In my own Christian life, I am seriously motivated by three things. Firstly, there is the fact that God demonstrated, and continues to reveal, his own unique and unconditional love for me as an individual, even while I continue to be a sinner. He sent his only begotten Son, Jesus Christ, into this world to die for my many sins —unconditionally! This is a truth that I still find difficult to grasp, that the great Creator God should love someone like me to such an extent. Secondly, I am motivated by the belief in the imminent return of the Lord Jesus Christ. The world must know that there is a remedy to life that will bring peace, guilt–free living, and a real hope. There are millions, perhaps billions, who have not yet heard the 'Good News'. My third motivator lurks within my conscious mind. Every now and then I have this thought: I am in the throne room of heaven, and thousands of people are being brought before the great white throne for judgement and condemnation. As I draw closer to see what is going on, I see a man whom I know. He is now before the one true Judge and about to be cast out. He turns to me with the most awful expression of pain and cries out to me, *'Why did you never tell me?'* This was an illustration used at

---

[1] *In the Presence of my Enemies*, Gracia Burnham & Dean Merrill, Tyndale House Publishers Inc, Weaton, Illinois. ISBN 0842385762. Used by permission.

a meeting I attended many years ago, by a visiting preacher, and it has never left me.

The apostle Paul could say with confidence:

I have been crucified with Christ; it is no longer I who live, but Christ lives in me; and the life which I now live in the flesh I live by faith in the Son of God, who loved me and gave Himself for me.

Galatians 2:20

Where does Christ figure in our daily priorities? I know that work is a pressure cooker environment; and there are so many urgent things to deal with, both at work and at home —and you deal with the urgent things that seek to grasp your attention, right now! The important matter waits quietly for you to call it into your life; the longer you wait for the right moment, the more your peace seems to suffer. Why not, from time to time, take your foot off the accelerator of life for just a moment. Ease off, '**be still**', and know the peace that only God can bring!

Christians at work should be motivated by the gospel and their own salvation, as well as hoping for and expecting the return of Christ. We should have a real desire to work for the cause of the gospel, seeing this as our 'greater work' which does have significant eternal consequences and rewards. It is greater than the denominational differences. Truly redeemed people, who believe in the propitiatory death of the Lord Jesus Christ for our sins and the infallibility of the Bible, should not see their differences as an excuse for failing to work together in the promotion of the gospel of our Lord Jesus Christ. This is a call for like-minded, Bible believing Christian people to labour in the same vineyard which, for many, is the world of work.

The opportunity and the need to share the gospel has never been greater. In less than ten years, trends which had already become established within many businesses— downsizing, globalisation, consolidation, diversification, reversion to core business—have become much more rapid programmes of continual change. A communications revolution has brought the world closer together. Things are now much more urgent than they used to be; and many are in a great hurry, it seems, to fill their lives with the busy-ness of work. Some of the most famous business names have vanished forever, others are much reduced, and companies have been taken over, merged and redefined. The phrase 'job security' no longer exists. Speaking recently to a man who worked as a coffin maker, he told me that he had only a temporary contract of employment. So even the most dependable businesses no longer give assurance of employment! At the centre of all of this change are people who have had their lives turned upside down by these activities. They need to hear about Christ! They need to hear about the peace that only he can bring into their troubled lives.

Many people have been moved around, and many have experienced voluntary or compulsory redundancy. Others have been moved sideways or been given job change options. Being a Christian at work has not protected anybody from these vocational volcanoes, but it has presented a glorious opportunity for Christian witness in the workplace. People are hungry for answers; we can tell them that Christ IS the answer!

The idea of writing this book was not originally mine. A number of people wanted copies of the various materials which have been used in my workplace and church presentations and seminars. I have therefore tried to re-present the work in a written format, both here and in companion publications of Bible studies and resources. Whilst I am writing about matters which are of great significance for Christians in the workplace, I trust that these things will be helpful to Christian people wherever they are.

I realize that this book is not exhaustive, nor is it intended to be a theological treatise, but I have attempted to include as much information as possible which would help to enable the reader to become an effective witness at work. I recognise the limitations of human frailty, and the need for the reader both to ensure that his or her walk with the Lord is real, and to understand that it is the word of God, working in harmony with the Spirit of God, that draws people to Jesus. We are merely the human agents of a loving God whose revealed will is to save the lost.

The book is dedicated to all of the many members, friends and supporters of the organisation and charity *Christians at Work*, especially those who labour day by day to live out their faith in the mission field that we call work.

1

THE JOURNEY BEGINS —YOUR CHOICES

The fundamental truth is that life is a journey. Where we pass through on the journey is not of itself the most important thing. What truly matters is where we **ultimately** end up, and at what stage in our life we determine our destination —our final destination. That is what really counts. Our response to Christ may have been affected by where the journey has taken us, day by day. Perhaps your journey has been awful and painful. For others it may have been a roller coaster ride, and for some a gentle stroll through life. But there comes a moment when we are confronted with the gospel; we become aware of the life, death and resurrection of our Saviour, Jesus Christ in a new, life–changing way.

I recall talking to Ed Hinds some years ago, when he was with New Tribes Mission at their former Matlock Bible School. He had been teaching students how to communicate the vital truths of the gospel, and part of the training involved door to door visitation work. Along with a couple of students, he had visited the home of a very wealthy man. He was a charming person and invited them into his house, but sadly for all the wrong reasons. He showed them his vast wealth and possessions. His point was simple: Why do I need Christ?

—I lack nothing! He had missed the point, and had no interest in what would happen to him after death. The truth is that this is the response of many people these days, and I suspect that we Christians are largely to blame. People often see nothing in us that they want. We have lost our ability to infect those around us with our love, joy, peace, patience, gentleness, goodness, faithfulness, meekness and self-control —the fruit of the Spirit; the characteristics of Christlikeness.

In everything there has to be a starting point, so here is the first question: Where have we come from; where did the journey start?

The text of the apostle Paul's letter to the Ephesians will feature prominently throughout this book, especially chapter two, verses one to ten.

And you He made alive, who were dead in trespasses and sins, in which you once walked according to the course of this world, according to the prince of the power of the air, the spirit who now works in the sons of disobedience, among whom also we all once conducted ourselves in the lusts of our flesh, fulfilling the desires of the flesh and of the mind, and were by nature children of wrath, just as the others. But God, who is rich in mercy, because of His great love with which He loved us, even when we were dead in trespasses, made us alive together with Christ, (by grace you have been saved), and raised us up together, and made us sit together in the heavenly places in Christ Jesus, that in the ages to come He might show the exceeding riches of His grace in His kindness toward us in Christ Jesus.

For by grace you have been saved through faith, and that not of yourselves: it is the gift of God, not of works, lest anyone should boast. For we are His workmanship, created in Christ Jesus for good works, which God prepared beforehand that we should walk in them.

I find this a delightful and yet extremely challenging passage of Scripture. Why? Because in ten verses Paul tells us exactly where we came from, what great things God has done for us, and what he has in store for us. He reminds us that before we came to Christ we were at war with God. We were driven by the lust of this world, disobedient, doomed to a lost eternity, dead in trespass and sin; and then, in verse four, we have those precious two words: 'But God'. These two words are God's message of unconditional love to a lost world, for they transcend our hopeless past and bring us into our hope–filled present and future. Previously, sin had worked against us; there was nothing that we could accomplish in our own strength. Now, because of God's unconditional love, mercy and grace, he can work in us and through us! But the word is 'can', because we humans are a fairly wilful and fickle lot and we have the ability to make choices. We will look at the issue of choice later.

Knowing that God has redeemed us from a lost eternity, that he will keep us because he adopted us into his family, and then one day is going to exalt us together with Christ, should in itself be a significant motivator, because we know, if we are truly honest, that there is actually nothing in us that makes us worthy; it is God who alone has made us worthy.

THE GOOD WORKS THAT WE SHOULD WALK IN....

In the July 2002 edition of **WorkWise** magazine, Mark Greene asks PA Claire Norgate a simple but very powerful question: 'How do you bring your faith to work?'

Her answer is as simple as the question, but yet it gives us a profound truth to ponder on: 'You know who you are before God; you're the same everywhere.'

Oh, how I pray that this would be the truth for all of us. I spend much of my life today visiting and speaking to Christian fellowship groups in their workplaces, and when I am not doing that I am usually at churches, speaking and, hopefully, challenging people to support and encourage those who work, to be effective in their Christian witness at work. But what I am seeing, all too often, is Christians with a sense of defeat. Changing work patterns, uncertainties and increased pressure to achieve more and more, are all conspiring to bring about an awful sense of being overpowered, overwhelmed and defeated by the turbulent world of work.

However, it is in these times of turmoil, testing and trials that we can really bring our Christian witness to the fore. The current atmosphere of political correctness in a post–Christian, postmodern, pluralistic society prohibits direct evangelism in many places of work. But there are other ways!

All too often, however, we find that this profound sense of defeat leads to a self destructive feeling of apathy, which in turn reinforces the sense of defeat! That cycle can go around and around continually, until we become totally blind to opportunity. It is true! We see opportunities literally fly before us, and because of our human tendency to be fickle, we stand back. We fear the response of those we seek to help. We are concerned about what people think about us because being friendly and helpful can be seen as a sign of weakness, and weakness has no place in today's workplace. The list of excuses that allows apathy to rule can be lengthy. But whether we like it or not, the excuses are evidence of selfishness, and selfishness is sin.

God's love is unconditional and free. He cannot tolerate the presence of sin and he knows your very nature. He knows that you are a sinner, but in his mercy he does not treat you as you deserve. In his grace he has given you what you do not deserve —unconditional love! In that love, he sent his only begotten Son, Jesus, to die for your sins. If that does not motivate you, consider the very nature of God, as briefly set out in John chapter three, verse thirty six:

> He who believes in the Son has everlasting life: and he who does not believe the Son shall not see life; but the wrath of God abides on him.

It was Paul who put it very bluntly when writing to the church at Corinth,

> Knowing, therefore, the terror of the Lord, we persuade men....
>
> *2 Corinthians 5:11a*

Paul was under no misapprehension concerning the holy and righteous nature of God; yes, God is a God of love, but indeed a terror to the unrepentant.

When we accept the Lord Jesus Christ as our Saviour and Lord, and come to terms with the greatness of what he has done for us ('That in the ages to come He might show the exceeding riches of His grace in His kindness toward us in Christ Jesus', Ephesians 5:7), he *can* work in us and through us for his glory. In Ephesians 2:10, Paul makes it very clear that God has a purpose for our lives. He has prepared a plan, and so we become a people who have a destiny. I am not referring only to our eternal destiny, but a living destiny in this present world, that becomes the evidence of our faith in Christ!

The trouble with a living destiny is that it can be ignored or plucked away if we let that happen, and the old destiny vulture—Satan, the devil—roosts in a tree nearby with a very contented smile. He cannot deprive us of our eternal destination, but he sure can hinder us from pointing others to our glorious hope, and spoil our witness—unless we resist him!

WHERE ARE WE GOING?

If we are absolutely honest about our Christian lives, I think we should all agree that one of the biggest problems is apathy. Many of us (myself included) have wasted too much time in becoming experts in apathy! So let us examine some of the things that may be hindering us. Perhaps some of these things are hurdles that we have allowed Satan to place before us:

WHAT ARE THE BARRIERS AND HINDRANCES IN YOUR DAILY LIFE? IS A LITTLE PRUNING NEEDED?

We all have habits: some good, some bad; we have hobbies and pastimes —again, some good and some bad. We have too many things that can supplant God in our lives. Every now and then we need to review our lives. If the television is one of your things, perhaps you have seen one of the bank advertisements which suggest that we all need a personal review.

Every year there is a particular time when my wife and I have to walk around our garden, looking at the plants and pruning them back where necessary. The process is needed at other times during the year, too. We prune back the leaves so that each tree will put all of its energy into the blossom, and so bear fruit.

We, too, need pruning, cutting back, from time to time, and we need to remove those things that hinder the living destiny that God has planned for us. I do not doubt for one moment that many of the things which preoccupy us can be very wholesome indeed. But the danger arises when 'the tail wags the dog'. We begin to find that our spiritual priorities are back to front. A 'spiritual life review' is something that we should indulge in on a fairly regular basis. Review your priorities!

WHAT IS YOUR DREAM? DO YOU HAVE VISION? WHERE ARE THE THINGS OF GOD IN YOUR SCALE OF VALUES?

These are questions that we should ask of ourselves almost every day. In one of the early writings of Charles Swindoll, he talks about the tyranny of the urgent —an apt and memorable expression. As humans we tend always to respond to the loudest and most urgent cry, yet that cry may not really be as urgent as it sounds. The other side of this is that we often create our own 'urgent' situations which are not in reality urgent at all —but we do like to appear very busy before the world! Whilst we are dealing with these supposedly urgent and distracting issues, the truly important thing is waiting quietly for us to get back to it! That is how it is for many Christians, yet, while we hesitate, time is slipping by and more souls are descending into a lost and awful eternity. That lost time can never be recovered!

So again, I ask the question: Where is the Saviour in your list of priorities? Those who work for larger companies or public sector organisations will have spent lots of time attending courses which seek to instil into your mind the wonders and glory of ABC plc or Ministry of Wot Nots, Managing for Excellence, Best Practice, Best Value, World Standard Quality & Performance, and so on —and you go back to your workplace invigorated by these presentations (or perhaps not!) But where are your 'standards of excellence', 'best practice' or 'world standard quality and performance' in your Christian life? Some years ago, when I was at Garforth Evangelical Church in Leeds, we were carrying out a major refurbishment of the building, part of which involved the construction of a new toilet area. One Saturday morning I was asked to take the joiner to our timber suppliers, to buy some laminated chipboard for the toilet cubicles. Have you ever bought white laminate board? How many sheets did you buy that had small chips or imperfections? On that Saturday morning my joiner friend would not accept one single sheet unless it was free of blemishes and chips! Only the best was good enough for the Lord, he would say to the warehouse foreman, so we had every sheet out until we had eight 2240 mm by 1220 mm boards that were as near perfect as possible. I know it all sounds ridiculous and, yes, it was embarrassing. But he was right. Where is God in our scale of values —high and glorified, or just *there*, in between all of the other 'urgent' things of life? Do we give him the fag end of our day and talents?

When Paul wrote to the Corinthians, he sought to bring harmony to a group of Christian people who clearly were struggling with many aspects of their fellowship. At the end of 1 Corinthians 12 he says, 'But earnestly desire the best gifts. And yet I show you a more excellent way.' He then sets out the supreme excellence of love in the life of the Christian. Do you strive for excellence in the way in which you demonstrate the love of God in your life?

WHAT ARE YOUR LIFE PRIORITIES?
HOW DO YOU FEEL ABOUT ETERNITY?

What is the most important thing that you do each day? Tell your spouse that you love them, hug the kids and let them know just how important and loved they are —fine! But do you spiritually embrace God every day? Do you tell him how much you love him? Do you give him the day, every day? And, yes, what do you think about eternity? When I was a foolish young man, I might have said that when I get to heaven I shall have a long list of questions: So who is right about this or that controversy? What about the millennium? And what about the rapture? —and a host of other matters I wondered about. As you grow in faith and years, you realize that eternity **IS** heaven, and these questions will have no place there. Eternity in heaven is going to be the most wonderful experience imaginable. No matter what good times we may have experienced here on earth, heaven will be immeasurably better. There we are going to be rewarded according to the way we treated and valued our salvation — *worked out* our salvation. (Note: we have not *earned* our salvation by works, for God's grace alone can save, not works). So consider this: is your life—your visible witness—demonstrating your faith? Is eternity a living reality for you? Then remember again that those you failed to warn may well be spending eternity in a place of eternal torment and damnation!

WHERE IS YOUR SAVIOUR WHEN YOU ARE AT WORK? IS HE SOMETIMES A BIT OF AN INCONVENIENCE?

When I thought about this, my first reaction was to discount it. How can I possibly say, 'Is it inconvenient to be a Christian?' The truth is that it is a question which I personally cannot ignore. During my time in business, especially as a young Christian, there were often times when this thought, in one form or another, crossed my mind. When honesty, morality and integrity issues arose, which required a response from me, I hesitated so often. If I do not do such and such, will it affect my career options? Why do rude jokes seem funny? —But I know I must not show my awareness of that. Do I really have to miss out on some event because I know it is not the place for a Christian man to be? As I grew in faith, love and knowledge of my Lord Jesus Christ, these childish and sometimes petulant thoughts faded into oblivion. I realised that these issues could be a wonderful opportunity for witness, providing we deal with them in grace and not judgement.

The world of work can be such a corrupting place, for the young Christian especially. We can try to pretend that at work nobody from our church or fellowship can see us, but the Lord always has his hand outstretched toward us. These are the times when we can hold on to the promise of God, that he will never forsake us, nor leave us on our own.

DO YOU REALLY OWN HIM AS LORD OF YOUR LIFE? (PSALM 42:8) —THE GOD OF YOUR LIFE!

I recall some years ago, as a young Christian, reading Psalm 42. I cannot say that it was one of my favourites particularly, I think I just struggled with the biblical imagery of being like a young deer panting by the water brook. But then I read verse 8, and on this particular occasion it stood out for me as if it were written in bright neon colours: 'A prayer to the God of my life.' What fabulous words! I suddenly realised that my God was interested in me in a very personal and profound way. I had never doubted him as my God. I saw him more as the Father in heaven, the Father of my Saviour. Suddenly, I realised that he was personally interested in me and that I can have as much of MY God as I want, without depriving anybody else. He was really much more interested in me than I had understood —in a way that was even closer than my own earthly father had been. It was just this experience that led me to the point in my life where I could say: yes, praise the Lord; he is the Lord of my life. Have you come to that position yet?

So perhaps it is time that you prayerfully carried out that personal review of your life so far, because, as we will consider later, when we offer our service to God there are conditions. When we give ourselves to God for his service, he requires us to be holy.

Do not be unequally yoked together with unbelievers. For what fellowship has righteousness with lawlessness? And what communion has light with darkness? And what accord has Christ with Belial? Or what part has a believer with an unbeliever? And what agreement has the temple of God with idols? For you are the temple of the living God. As God has said:

> "I will dwell in them
> and walk among them.
> I will be their God,
> And they shall be My people."

Therefore

> "Come out from among them
> And be separate, says the Lord."

2 Corinthians 6:14–17a

Pretty powerful stuff! But this is where we are supposed to be. The inescapable fact is that what was good and right for Christians almost two thousand years ago is still applicable today. Yes, we are forgiven and redeemed in his sight, but are we living holy lives? And is our life acceptable before God? To aim for anything less is clearly inadequate — we would be living beneath our privileges as his children!

PREPARING FOR THE JOURNEY....

Let us examine three important statements from the word, which may encourage us on our way as we prepare for our journey without fear of attack from the 'destiny vulture'.

I can do all things through Christ who strengthens me.

Philippians 4:13

As I travel from place to place, I quite often enjoy the privilege of hospitality in a Christian home. They tell me that ladies love to look at other people's soft furnishings. For myself, as long as there is good food and a comfortable bed somewhere, I could not give a hoot about the soft furnishings. But I do like to see the texts that different people have on their wall plaques and bookcases, and I am sure that this text is one of the most popular. But it is also one of those wonderful texts that we can take for ourselves, and own. Christ *strengthens me*. It is not one of those woolly statements, is it? It is dynamic; there is a source of energy in the very words, and they are there for everyday use, both in the big things and the small issues of life. We can be assured that if we are living and working in the light of his presence, and walking in his will, then he will take us over the hurdles that stand in our way, if we allow him to do so; and not just the hurdles but also the opportunities as they arise before us.

For with GOD, all things are possible.

Mark 10:27

I really like this text, which is the second one for us to remember in our preparation for the journey —principally because of who said it and what he said before it. They are the words of our Lord Jesus Christ himself: 'With men it is impossible, but not with God....' We are not to doubt his word. Doubt and lack of assurance are two of the biggest hindrances to living the Christian life and witness. Again, we have to remember that there is one who would rather see us indulging in self satisfying social activities rather than seeking to share the love of God with those around us. Satan is our enemy, he is the enemy of God, he has lost us, but that does not mean that he has given up on us. If you have doubt in your mind concerning the reality of salvation, or the ability of God to do anything according to his word and promises, then be assured that the orator trying to speak to your mind who wants to confirm your doubt is Satan. Just remember how our Lord himself dealt with these issues when he came under temptation in the wilderness. He used the word of God:

...Man shall not live by bread alone, but by every word of God.

Luke 4:4b

...You shall worship the LORD your God, and Him only you shall serve.

Luke 4:8b

...You shall not tempt the LORD your God.

Luke 4:12b

That same ability to use the word of God in spiritual warfare is available to you and me. Never doubt what God's word can do!

**Trust in the LORD with all your heart,
and lean not on your own understanding;
in all your ways acknowledge Him,
And He shall direct your paths.**
Proverbs 3:5–6

This, the third key text for our preparation, is possibly the most abused passage in the entire Bible. We human beings are a fickle lot. When I was a young Christian, one of our elders suggested that I should perhaps help with some door to door visitation, inviting people to a special event at the church. I churned inwardly. I tried desperately to ring around some business friends to arrange an 'unavoidable' meeting for that night —but guess what, everybody was busy then. So the night came, and after the first twenty minutes or so I found myself happily doing what I was doing! It is the fear of the unknown that frightens us. It is even more difficult at work, because you cannot just get up and move along. Once you have set your hand to the plough you must keep on to the end of the furrow, and the three key preparatory texts we have looked at give us assurance that all things are possible with God. Another verse I often claim for myself is from Psalm 31:15, '*My times are in Your hand,*' When we give our time to the Lord, it is amazing just how wonderfully life works out!

But remember this, as we yield to the Lord and we see things working out, we have a great human temptation to sit back and say, 'didn't WE do well.' So remember this:

The things achieved in our lives are not made possible by any effort of yours or mine, but because of what God has done for us through his Son, our Lord and Saviour Jesus Christ. Christ is the real hero! To him is due ALL the glory!

Certainly, we are to work in co-operation with him and

obedience to him, but we can claim no credit or glory for ourselves; any good we do is his new creation at work in us, and we are not independent, but rather we are members of his body, subordinate to Christ, our head.

The God we worship and love is supernatural. He defies the world's expectation. His thoughts are not like man's thoughts, and his ways are not our ways. The things that he requires of us certainly do not conform to the ideals which this world finds acceptable. So how do we move forward in his power? Well, let me give you three more worthy texts from the word to take to heart, but first allow me to remind you again of the importance of avoiding that **tyranny of the urgent** which I mentioned earlier. Once we have our hand upon the plough, or even before we have the horse hitched, you can almost guarantee that some trifling issue will come to distract us from the task laid out before us by God. It always happens. The devil, that old deceiver and liar, will do his utmost to distract us from our true purpose. Resist him! Give that problem over to the Lord, and he will direct your path.

THREE PRIORITIES

These next three texts concern some priorities that we need to lay hold of before we start ploughing the furrow, and I have to stress now that, by the world's standards, these proposals seem unnatural and even strange:

SUPPLICATION — PRAYER

The effective, fervent prayer of a righteous man avails much.

James 5:16b

We often seem to forget that when we come to Christ we are not only given a new life, but we are also given tremendous power. By this I mean the power of prayer. On my bookshelf I have six small volumes on prayer by E. M. Bounds. written over a hundred years ago, yet so relevant for this day in which we live. He writes about the purpose, possibilities and power of prayer, and about using prayer as a weapon, illustrating this teaching from Scripture. When we pray, God works in often surprising places. He works powerfully in the lives of those around us, those whom we love, and those we work with —and, of course, those who perhaps we do not like so much! Are you, perhaps, among those many Christians whose experience of prayer has been a little like having a new car: at first you want to sit in it and drive it around at every opportunity, but when the novelty wears off you use it only when you have to? Yet if we pray fervently and effectively in God's will, he really will do great things for his glory. He will work in areas where we never expected him to work, and change things we scarcely believed could change. Above all, people's lives will be changed when we pray!

SUBMISSION TO THE WILL OF GOD

I beseech you therefore, brethren, by the mercies of God, that you present your bodies a living sacrifice, holy, acceptable to God, which is your reasonable service.

Romans 12:1

Often in the workplace we talk about company mission statements and the claims they make upon their employees. One word that you will not find in a company mission statement is 'submission'. But God, who demonstrated his love toward us by sending his son to die for us, even while we were still sinners, does make a demand upon us which he considers to be not unreasonable! When you realize that it was Jesus, God incarnate, who died that awful death on the cross for your sins, then it no longer seems to be in any way unreasonable that we should offer our abilities and talents for his unconditional use. It may help, as you read that verse, to associate that word 'holy' with the word 'wholly'! We are to offer ourselves wholly to him; and we are 'holy' because he has set us apart for himself. Moreover, because by grace, through faith, we received Jesus as our Saviour, we are wholly acceptable to him. We need to have a holy life. Our lives are to be marked by holy living. We are set apart for God's service, and we therefore set ourselves apart from 'the world' whilst still being in it. Thus we are to come to him with clean hands. God cannot use us if we are being double minded about our adherence to the values he has established for us to live by, in his word.

SURRENDER TO BE LIKE THE LORD JESUS

Let each of you look out not only for his own interests, but also for the interests of others. Let this mind be in you which was also in Christ Jesus.

Philippians 2:4–5

Christlikeness should be the goal. Let me tell you a story about my visit to the headquarters of one of our larger banks. When I visit a workplace fellowship group, we often meet in either a conference room or small meeting room. Once I attended such a meeting in a large cupboard (literally!) under the stairs! But on this occasion we met in the bank's main boardroom —and how palatial that was. I did not have to spend time setting up the computer and projector for the usual PowerPoint presentation; I merely plugged the computer into the floor socket, and the end wall of the boardroom came alive!

The group was the usual mixed bunch of folk from every level within the organisation. However, I noticed that at the far end of the table sat a man with a very dignified countenance. The suit he wore was probably equal in value to a year, or perhaps two, of my income! He did not say much during the meeting, but afterwards, when we were talking, I noticed that on each wrist beneath the immaculately ironed white cuffs of his shirt there were two sweat bands. On one it said, 'What would Jesus say?' On the other was written, 'What would Jesus do?' He told me that he was the Financial Director of one of the operational boards of the bank, and that he often had to write reports both to the operational board and the PLC board concerning both lending and continuing support for the bank's customers. Sometimes the information he had to impart was good and sometimes it was bad. He said that the message on the sweat bands reminded him, as he wrote his report, to pray and bring God into the matter, because often his recommendation could have a devastating effect upon the lives of people.

Sadly for that bank's customers, this godly man has since retired, but it was wonderful to find a man at that level of seniority in the business world submitting so openly to the will of God and striving to be like his Saviour.

Do we seek for Christlikeness in our daily lives? Remember this: the fruit of the spirit, those nine key components for effective Christian living, are nothing less than the characteristics of Christ himself, and that we are to allow

ourselves to be transformed into his likeness. That transformation should be our life's goal and purpose. It is the
work of the Holy Spirit within the believer, and he calls us to
co-operate with him in this work. As Paul wrote:

> But we all, with unveiled face, beholding as in a mirror
> the glory of the Lord, are being transformed into the
> same image from glory to glory, just as by the Spirit of
> the Lord.
>
> *2 Corinthians 3:18*

Always remember, too, that you are not on your own as
you pursue this objective, for God makes available to us his
own resources. As Patrick Whitworth writes in his book
Becoming Fully Human:

> All Christians are people following Jesus... with his
> guidance (wisdom) and help (the Holy Spirit), with a
> permanent safety net for their ongoing failures (the
> cross), and a hope that one day the struggle will give
> way to bliss (heaven).[1]

---

[1] *Becoming Fully Human*, Patrick Whitworth, Terra Nova
Publications. ISBN 1901949230. Used by permission.

2

Safety Checks
Before We Depart...

DO WE REALLY HAVE CONFIDENCE?

So, having taken hold of the truths of Scripture that we looked at in the last chapter, we are inwardly assured that all things are possible and we understand the importance of supplication, submission and surrender —but do we have confidence?

On those rare Saturdays I spend at home these days, I do not enjoy being disturbed by those bright eyed young men who come to my door brimming with confidence in a most untrustworthy and false doctrine. Every time, they pull out this beautifully leather bound King James Bible and ask the same question: do I believe it to be the word of God? Of course, I can say that I certainly do! Then they introduce a smaller leather bound book, the Book of Mormon, and their next question runs along these lines: 'Sir, is it not reasonable to believe that God gave us another word for our times?'

At this point we start to talk about the Bible, our Saviour, his relationship with the heavenly Father; and we range all over the place. But they cling on with absolute confidence to their false doctrine. They always remain calm and polite and will even agree to come and talk to you later about these things —though they never turn up! Despite everything, they are never lacking in confidence, like the Jehovah's Witnesses who deny essential revealed Christian doctrines, including the divinity of Jesus. So it is quite possible to be genuinely, sincerely confident in a matter of faith, yet at the same time to be absolutely mistaken.

The problem with being an evangelical Christian is that so often, when we start talking about our faith to anybody, at some stage, we seem to feel a lack of confidence. The reassuring thing is that it was the same for some of God's mightiest prophets and leaders. But our confidence is founded not on feelings but on God's self-revelation.

DO YOU HAVE CONFIDENCE IN THE BIBLE AS THE WORD OF GOD?

All Scripture is given by inspiration of God, and is profitable for doctrine, for reproof, for correction, for instruction in righteousness, that the man of God may be complete, thoroughly equipped for every good work.

2 Timothy 3:16–17

It bothers me greatly that many who would call themselves evangelicals fail to affirm biblical inerrancy. But such a denial of God's revelation is like building a house on sand. If we cannot agree on the inerrancy of the Scriptures, we have no basis for our faith and doctrines but are, in effect, suggesting that the Bible is merely the words of well-intentioned men.

DO YOU HAVE CONFIDENCE IN THE WORK OF THE HOLY SPIRIT —THAT HE WILL FILL YOU, RENEW YOU AND EMPOWER YOU?

"And I will pray the Father, and He will give you another Helper, that He may abide with you forever —the Spirit of truth, whom the world cannot receive, because it neither sees Him nor knows Him; but you know Him, for He dwells with you and will be in you."

John 14:16–17

There are differing views in the Christian world concerning the work and gifts of the Spirit. However, there is one thing that we should all be agreed upon: it is he who indwells us, empowers us, and makes us bold when that is needed for the purposes of the gospel. Again, we depend not on our own ideas or feelings but on the very promise of our Lord and Saviour Jesus Christ.

DO YOU HAVE CONFIDENCE IN PRAYER?

We have access by faith into this grace.

Romans 5:2

I suppose most of us would agree that Romans 5 contains some of the most revealing statements concerning our relationship with God through our Lord Jesus Christ. In 1974, I had been involved with the design and development of what was then called the Castle Centre in Stockton on Teesside, and The Queen was coming to open it. About three weeks prior to the big day, a gentleman appeared, a very military type; he had come to coach us in how to conduct ourselves in the presence of Her Majesty. We spent almost all day being told not to speak unless we are spoken to. On no account should we touch her. The most memorable thing was being told that if The Queen spoke to us—and the likelihood of that was almost negligible for insignificant people like us— we were to address her as, "Mam as in jam, not Marm as in arm!" What a hassle! You and I have access into the presence of our mighty and wonderful God who is above all powers and principalities, in the twinkling of an eye. All that we have to do is call out to him, and we are there. Do you have confidence in your communication—your prayer life—with God?

If we go along with everything thus far, then we are ready to begin, so where do we start in this uncertain, politically correct, world of ours. Let me suggest to you that **friendship** is the best place to begin.

THE PROBLEM WITH FRIENDSHIPS

Having a real friend is fine, but it can be more onerous than you can possibly imagine. Why? Because true friendship requires absolute honesty; honesty about the good things in life and honesty about the not so good things, too —honesty about both success and failure. It is relatively easy to share good news with our friends, but it is not always easy to share bad news. But our attitude of friendship should help to communicate our faith to others. This is where the fruit of the Spirit really should show itself working: in our day–to–day lives.

In all that follows in this book, and in the companion set of Bible Studies, there is a very specific purpose: to help Christians, who for the most part work amongst others who are not Christians, to consider their situation and responsibility in the light of biblical teaching. Yes, I know that sounds rather dry for the third millennium! But the resounding truth of God's revelation of himself and his purposes, as recorded in his word which is the same yesterday, today and for ever, is absolutely central and is at the heart of what we are about.

Three key things will become clear in the course of our journey of exploration of the word of God: our objective standing in relationship to our Father God through our Lord Jesus Christ; our response within this relationship, when we have become aware of how deep and meaningful it truly is; and, finally, our responsibility to allow the Holy Spirit to work in and through us. If you attend a church where you are well taught in the truths of the Scriptures, you will find nothing novel in any of that. But I hope that you will be seriously challenged as to our Christian duty, to work out our salvation. (No, I did not say work *toward* or work *for* our salvation, for this is the free gift of God. Works are simply the evidence of that salvation.)

One of the problems with a free gift is that we do not always appreciate it as much as something that we have earned for ourselves, and therefore we may be tempted to undervalue it. Much depends, however, upon one's personal circumstances and attitude. I suspect that *naturally* I am a fairly apathetic person. Well, I don't suspect it, I know it! So from time to time I need to be pushed and prodded in the right direction. I have been a Christian long enough also to realize that I am not unique in this. Does that give me any comfort? Certainly not! What shocks and shames me is that I can so often take my salvation for granted. I forget the price that was paid; I forget the hope that I have been given by a loving God, who demonstrated his own unique love for me by sending his only begotten Son, Jesus, to die for my sins. From time to time we all need a refresher! Above all, we need to be aware of and faithful to our precious friendship with Jesus, whose word to us never fails. As we seek to develop ministries based on friendship with others, never let us forget the vital reality of the friendship with him which he made possible, as he declared:

You are My friends if you do whatever I command you.
John 14:14

3

LESSONS FROM A BOAT
—BOLDNESS!

I live a strange sort of life. Although I live in Northumberland, by the sea, my work base is Rugby and I get to visit most parts of the country during the working year. Thankfully, I do get home for some part of almost half the weekends. So there I was one Saturday morning. My wife was at work. I was doing the washing and ironing, thinking about my commitments for the coming week. The television happened to be on in the background, and they were showing a programme about the 'BT Global Challenge, Round the World Yacht Race'. Teams of people had paid huge sums of money to spend nine months trying to enjoy themselves—or to risk life and limb on boats, as it seemed to me! I stopped to watch and listen as the crews were being interviewed at the halfway stage. Common to nearly all of the interviewees was the answer, 'I've learned a lot about myself.'

Interesting things do indeed happen in boats, and I have always been intrigued by the way in which some of the most important lessons learned in Scripture were given in and around the water. We are now going to think about some of those lessons — I call them 'boat stories'.

Our first boat story is to be found at the end of the fourth chapter of the Gospel of Mark. The Lord Jesus had just finished speaking to his followers, and was ready to head back across the Sea of Galilee. Jesus, tired now it was evening, got into the back of the boat and fell asleep. The disciples climbed aboard the boat, and they headed out to sea.

After a short time, a terrible storm developed. Apparently that was not an unusual occurrence on the Sea of Galilee, but this storm was much worse than normal. The wind was whistling through the rigging. The waves were crashing over the bows of the boat. The disciples thought: This is it, we are going to die! It was a measure of the storm's power that they really did expect to perish there out at sea. Turning to look toward the stern, they could see the Lord Jesus, sound asleep, not in the least affected by the storm.

Perhaps as you read this, you feel that you too are going through some dire circumstances. I am reminded of a time when I was flying in a thunderstorm, from Cardiff to Leeds/Bradford Airport. It was just one of those funny little aeroplanes, a Short 330, with a few seats, no pressurization; the weather was so bad that we were flying at just three thousand feet. The pilot was following the lights of the M4, the M5 and then the M6, and when we got near Manchester, he literally turned right to follow the M62 to Leeds. He sounded so calm, as if this sort of thing happened twice a day. I could tell from the faces of my fellow passengers that most of us were terrified!

Something rather similar was happening here. The disciples were absolutely terrified, fearing for their lives. As for the Lord Jesus. he was sound asleep. But you can do that when you are the one who spoke creation into being! The disciples woke him up. I suspect that was not because they thought he could do anything, but because they were desperate for any kind of help or direction at this point. Jesus awoke and simply spoke to the storm three words: **"Peace. Be still."** I used to say something like this to our children all day long sometimes, but nothing ever seemed to happen. Jesus said it *just once* to the storm and it abated immediately. Imagine that! What amazing power: the power of God. When all is quiet again, he asked the disciples, "Why are you so fearful? How is it that you have no faith?"

Our lives can be like that storm on the Sea of Galilee —it may not necessarily be a physical storm, but simply the circumstances which surround us that can be so frightening. It may be that deadlines are not being met at work; there might be panic because of some error, or concerns about changing working practices. At home it can be anything from a lack of money or a problem with the children —and how we long for peace and security!

Can you imagine how the disciples were feeling after that incident? Perhaps they felt a little foolish for having said anything to Jesus in the first place. But if at first they were terrified by the storm, they now had an even more compelling reason to be concerned. Now they were just a little worried by this man, Jesus, who they had begun to follow; whose disciples they had become so relatively recently. Yes, they knew him to be a prophet and a teacher —a good man, capable of doing miracles, but here they had seen something of his tremendous power. So, *just who was this man, that with a few simple words he could calm a raging storm?*

I think I know how they felt about Jesus Christ. They were strangely drawn to him, yet at the same time rather frightened. Such ambivalence in our responses is not all that uncommon, and as children most of us will have experienced such a mixture of attraction accompanied by uncertainty in very ordinary situations. I remember how I felt about my first infant school teacher. As I remember it (and I was only five at the time) she seemed ancient, probably at least ninety! Whilst she was nice most of the time, she could also seem very alarming sometimes, and I recall that I was both drawn to her and frightened by her all at the same time. C. S. Lewis conveyed this double reaction with great literary impact. In his *Chronicles of Narnia*, Aslan the lion, a type of Christ, is the hero of the stories. The children are quite taken with him, but at the same time they are rather frightened of him as well. *After all, he is a lion.* And if he wanted to, he would be powerful enough to tear them limb from limb. As Lewis was fond of saying throughout the books, Aslan was not a tame lion. So now the disciples were discovering that their leader, Jesus, was more than they had suspected, and they really were in the midst of a dilemma.

So it was that when they had seen him quell the storm they became more fearful rather than less. They had seen a new dimension of the power of Jesus, and they said of him, "Who can this be, that even the wind and sea obey him?" They had been taught a vital lesson about God's authority over his own created order, and about the divine power of Jesus.

They had first been terrified of dying in the storm. That is characteristic of the most basic fear of human beings. We are naturally afraid of death —of losing ourselves before we ever really find ourselves. But they were not just afraid of dying. They were also afraid of life and all of its possibilities with this man who was also God—Jesus, who could calm a raging storm. They had become terrified of supernatural divine power, which they did not understand. So here we have the disciples — frightened of death; frightened by the perils of life; seemingly frightened even of God, whom they could not understand —and with a tendency to be frozen in fear. I suspect that this really was the point at which their discipleship got under way in earnest. They were coming to a realisation we all have to come to sooner or later: that life is not easy! Maybe this comes to you at the death of a loved one, or at your own brush with death, or when you graduate from university and you now realize you are on your own, or when you are fifty something and lose your job and seem to have no prospect of finding another.

Somewhere along the line it comes to all of us that we have been left out here in the middle of a great big ocean with a rickety old ship, a lousy rudder, no sails, and we have to make some sense out of this mess called life. The question then is not whether life is terrifying or not. The question is: what do you do in the face of life's terror? Do you allow it to defeat you? Do you run away from it? Or do you face it head on? What did the disciples do? Well, let us look at the next story from a boat.

Our second boat story comes from the moments shortly after Jesus had just fed five thousand people from a few loaves and fishes. The people had become so awed by him that they wanted to make Jesus become the new king of Israel. But his kingship was to be different from what they had in mind. He left them and went up into the mountains to be alone, first telling the disciples to cross the Sea of Galilee ahead of him.

You can imagine these men heading down to the harbour. They would not have understood the full significance of what was going on. But they followed Jesus' instructions. Once again, when they were well out at sea, having rowed for three or four miles this time, a terrible storm came upon them. But this time there was no Jesus asleep in the back of the boat. It seemed that they were on their own now. To make matters worse, what looked like a ghostly figure was walking toward them across the water. The figure spoke: **"Take courage! It is I. Don't be afraid."** (See Matthew 14:27 *NIV*.) I always thought courage was to step forward without any fear whatsoever. But it occurred to me that, in our experience, this may be stupidity rather than courage. Courage is stepping forward *despite* whatever fear you feel.

And Peter thought he had heard that voice before. He said, "Lord, if it's you... tell me to come to you on the water." How vital it is to be sure that it is the voice of the Lord we are hearing and ready to obey. Peter was right to check; we, too, need to know Jesus so well that we recognize his authentic word to us as his disciples.

The Lord Jesus simply replied, "Come."

So Peter got out of the boat and he walked on the water. Such trust! Such obedience! Have you ever done that? I have never done that. Did the rest of the disciples do that? No, they stayed back there in the boat. The only one who had the courage to get out of the boat and walk on the water was Peter. Oh sure, he subsequently took his eyes off Jesus, fell into the water, and cried, "Lord, save me." That

45

is an important point, of course: only by remaining attentive to Jesus can we stay afloat! But do not let us miss this vital lesson: Peter needed to be sufficiently courageous to get out of the boat and walk forward on the water, towards Jesus, in the first place.

One of the first key stages in life is to realize that life is difficult, problematic, even terrifying at times. That amazing miracle, in which Peter is enabled to 'do the impossible' when acting in obedience to a command of the Lord Jesus, shows us what the second vital stage of life is: it is having the courage to take a tiny little step of faith —moving forward, even in the face of life's fear.

I am reminded of our daughter, Catherine, who decided that she would go to Kidderminster to do her nursing training. She was, without doubt, a 'home bird'; you just could not stop her from clinging to the apron strings of home! Then she went, and within two years, having made that all–important first step toward independence, 'getting out of the boat', she found herself, as it were, 'walking on water'. Now she is 6,000 miles away working for *New Tribes Mission* in Mexico. Many of us have rejoiced to see our grown–up children take some bold step, in response to the call of the Lord.

A few years ago, at a time when I was contemplating leaving secular employment for full time ministry, I was talking with a good friend of mine. I was considering how I could make this major change in my life. What if I could not handle the challenge? What if I were to take the risk and it were to prove to be too much for me? I had been there before, and knew that the consequences could be awesome! My friend simply said to me, "I've never known anyone who was broken by taking a risk, if the Lord's in it. I've never known anyone who was broken by accepting a godly challenge. The only way you'll be broken is if you don't allow the Lord to work out his will in your life. The only way you'll be broken is if your only decision is to remain indecisive." I suppose that was good advice. As it was, I did not have to make any decision. The Lord did it for me. Peter would have understood that.

He got out of the boat. He walked on the water. So we have another important lesson learnt in a boat: the key to walking on water lies in hearing and obeying the call of Jesus. Like Peter, make sure it is the Lord who is calling; then do what he says; and always keep your eyes on Jesus as you 'go for it' in obedience.

Finally, we have to look at the twenty seventh chapter of Acts for our third boat story. The apostle Paul was a prisoner. He was on his way to Rome to appear before Caesar. He had been transferred from one ship to another. He was now in a place called Fair Haven, and the vessel was preparing to set sail, bound for Phoenix.

Paul talked to the captain and owner of the ship, and suggested that it was not the best time of the year to undertake the journey by sea. But he was just a prisoner. Why should they take any particular notice of him? So they set sail and within three days were overtaken by a terrible storm. There were hurricane force winds to deal with. The captain realised that there was no possibility of making any headway against such terrible weather, so they furled the sails and battened everything down in order to ride out the storm. But that strategy did not work! After eight days the storm was still raging. The description of the scene in Acts is graphic and moving; we can almost imagine ourselves there —the panic, the fear and the danger are powerfully depicted. The crew started throwing things overboard — anything to keep the ship afloat. After eleven days, all 276 seasoned sailors aboard had lost hope.

So what did Paul do? We might have been cautious about what we would say, perhaps feeling that to exercise a measure of tact and diplomacy would be sensible in that devastating situation amongst so many distraught people, some of them heavily armed. But Paul bravely reminded them of his earlier warning. God blessed the apostle with many gifts, including boldness! "Men, you should have taken my advice not to sail from Crete, then you would have spared yourselves this damage and loss." (Acts 27:21b).

Again bravely, Paul went on to tell the captain and the

crew, "But now I urge you to keep up your courage, because not one of you will be lost; only the ship will be destroyed."

Once more we observe Paul's boldness and courage as he testifies as to how he had been told this would be the outcome: "Last night an angel of the God whose I am and whom I serve stood beside me and said, 'Do not be afraid, Paul. You must stand trial before Caesar; and God has graciously given you the lives of all who sail with you.'"

Can you imagine what it takes to stand up in front of 276 seasoned sailors and say that an angel has spoken to you? You can imagine the sailors hearing Paul's words. A degree of scepticism might have been likely to emerge! For whatever reason, though, they believed him. We learn, too, that they were now willing to take his advice.

They had not eaten in fourteen days, so Paul said, "Now I urge you to take some food. You need it to survive. Not one of you will lose a single hair from his head." Best of all, Paul then prayed in front of them. We learn that he took the bread and gave thanks. So they prayed and they ate.

They were hoping to run the ship aground onto the beach. But instead they ran aground into a sandbar. They assumed that everyone who was able to would swim for the island. Those who could not do so would wait for the ship to break up and ride to the shore on pieces of wreckage. Did it cause Paul any consternation when the soldiers planned to kill the prisoners in case they escaped? We are not told, but having seen his faith and boldness in action, and been made aware of his confidence in God's will for him to go to Rome, it seems most unlikely!

Most of us would have been extremely concerned, and perhaps more than a little fearful at the prospect of appearing before Caesar, the hazardous situation of the shipwreck, and the casualness with which the soldiers were willing to execute a group of people in custody.

But whether or not any fearful thoughts crossed Paul's mind, he had been able to testify boldly that an angel of God had spoken to him. He had confidently given wise and godly counsel to the commanding officer and to the assembled company. Then he had witnessed by praying before eating. Then, when he reached the safety of the island of Malta, what did he do? He risked his life preaching the gospel in that hostile territory. He even shook a poisonous snake off his hand into the fire! We marvel at the boldness, courage and obedient faith of Paul at every stage. We are not intended merely to admire what we read about here in the apostle's life, but to follow the example of his boldness and practical faith, exercised in real life situations. We see that he was always ready to witness to the supernatural power of God in both words and deeds. That is exactly what we are meant to be doing in our own daily lives. Paul's key to effective life and witness? —he knew Jesus personally, was thoroughly convinced of the power in the word of God, and was constantly open to the leading and in–filling of the Holy Spirit —and quick to obey. What a powerful example for us if and when we are trying to deal with timidity, fear and a sense of powerlessness!

So if, in the first stage of our Christian life, we find that life is becoming difficult, problematic perhaps, even at times terrifying, moving on to the second stage involves learning to take small steps of faith in the face of the circumstances, resisting the temptation to become fearful, and indeed repenting of any fear that begins to take root in our thinking —for in the Scriptures the command is always 'do not be afraid'. We are actually required by God to be bold in doing what he has told us clearly to do. So as we learn what it means to walk in obedience, we can see that it follows— and the example of Paul demonstrates this to us—that the third stage of life is like this: having taken so many of those little steps of faith forward, as we have grown in the knowledge and love of Jesus Christ, eventually we can boldly, confidently undertake bigger things for him, with bold leaps like those we see depicted so vividly in the powerful witness of Paul.

But the question remains for most of us: how do we get from point A—sometimes being terrified of death—terrified of life—terrified of a God we do not understand—to point C:

being able to take bold leaps forward for the cause of Christ? The answer is: in the same way Peter and Paul did — by taking a tiny step of faith forward, one step at a time. The early stages of Paul's Christian life prepared him for what was to follow later on, including that momentous and highly significant journey to Rome. God is preparing you and me for the next stage in his plan for our lives.

In practical terms, you might wake up in the morning and say, *"Today Lord, no matter how difficult, no matter how hard, I'm going to take a step of faith for your glory."* And then the next day you say, *"Today, Lord, I'm going to take another step of faith with you."* And you move slowly from point A, to point B, to point C, but then that does not mean some difficult circumstances will not come along, apparently sending you back to point A all over again. But you will not be right back where you started, because God will have been changing you, teaching you, strengthening you, and you will have been growing in his word as you have sought to apply it. The process of maturing will have been under way.

Christians are not exempt from tests and trials. But still go on making this declaration of your heart's desire and will to move forward in faith *today.* Get up and say *"Today, Lord; I'll take a step of faith today for you."* Hard? You bet it is hard. You know it is hard. But it is the way to live, if we place the proper value upon our salvation! When you received Jesus you became a new creation. You are now a temple of the Holy Spirit. The Lord dwells in you. You have died to sin and are alive to God. The power that raised Jesus from the dead is at work in you. You are not defenceless. The devil will have a go at you; he will try to fill your mind with doubts and fears, and seek to cause you to question your motives. But always recall that the command of God is to resist the devil; and the corresponding promise is that then, when you do so, the enemy will flee! Never forget that the power of God is much greater than the power of the devil.

During the mid 90s, I had a colleague at work who had a number of difficult things come into his life. His father had died unexpectedly of a disease that never was diagnosed, hard as the doctors tried. Then his daughter came down with a life–threatening illness. To make matters worse, my colleague had been diagnosed with a chronic stomach disease and by the end of the year he had to give up work permanently. When he was coming through it all, I asked him how he had hung on. He said, "There were a lot of times when I wanted to give up. Heaven knows I wanted to give up. But if I had given up I would have stopped the journey short. And I refused to stop the journey short. So I just keep living as the Lord tells us, just one day at a time. And I never look back, because you can never look back."

"As the Lord tells us...." That is the key my friend discovered and used. To know the word of God, to hear and obey it, is vital as we deal with the tougher things in life; and applying the word in the little everyday things now will prepare us for whatever is to come. We may not always get it right, but we will be equipped, as we put on the armour of God and remember that we are not facing attacks alone but with the one who died for us so that we might be cleansed from all sin and enjoy his presence for all eternity.

My colleague told me that he and his wife had bought a boat on Lake Windermere, and when possible they would go up there and just sail. He said they had both learned a lot by just sitting in a boat....

4

A VISIT TO THESSALONICA

When Paul's companion Timothy visited Thessalonica he was thrilled, and when he reported back to Paul we are told that Paul was much comforted by the report. We are also making just a brief visit to Thessalonica and hopefully we will be both thrilled and challenged. We do not have the space for a long and detailed visit; we are simply going to review some of the qualities of these first century believers and the relationship that Paul had with them.

The founding of the church in Thessalonica is one of the most exciting accounts in the Acts of the Apostles. Paul visited the city and, after just three weeks of his preaching and reasoning from the Scriptures, many people were drawn to put their faith in Christ, and a church came into being. The church started, however, with a riot. The Jews, filled with envy, did not in any way appreciate the gospel. So concerned were they, in fact, that they gathered together some of the local ruffians (the AV describes them so well as lewd fellows of the baser sort!) with the intention of driving Paul and his companions away. But Paul, being forewarned, escaped. Poor Jason, who had provided Paul with hospitality, was hauled before the city magistrate, and the primary charge said it all, "These who have turned the world upside down have come here too." (See Acts 17:6.) Jason was effectively bound over to keep the peace. It seems as though everywhere Paul went, in one way or another he left his mark.

When we read Paul's first letter to these new believers we see what it was that caused him to be much comforted. So what can we learn from these first century Christians?

In chapter one, Paul applauds those infant believers because of the way in which they had embraced the Lord Jesus Christ as their Saviour and Lord and, since they had grown in faith, he addressed them as being in God the Father and the Lord Jesus Christ. The evidence was their work of **faith**, their labour of **love** and their patience of **hope**. They were a saved people; the tares had not yet got amongst the wheat. So it was that Paul could address them as being in God and in the Lord Jesus Christ.

He applauds them also for being a people truly **surrendered** and so marked by **Christlikeness**. Paul writes, 'And you became followers of us and of the Lord…. (See 1 Thessalonians 2:6). Then he notes how they turned to God from idols to serve the living and true God. Thessalonica was only a few miles from Mount Olympus, a centre linked to the worship of mythical Greek deities, and this cultic life had a very strong hold upon the people of the area. We are then reminded that the Christians of Thessalonica were prepared to **suffer** for the sake of the gospel. For they, '…received the word with much affliction, with joy of the Holy Spirit'!

They also knew the importance of the gospel message itself. That they were truly **soul-winners** we know, because Paul comments on the way in which they sounded forth the truth from the platform of their changed lives; this had made such big news that Paul had already heard about it. The secret is in the words 'sounded forth' (v. 8). The root Greek word from which we get the words 'sounded forth' is the same word from which we also get the word 'echoed'. In other words, they sounded forth the truth of the pure gospel, undiluted by man!

They were also a **'second-coming'** church filled with expectant people. They were motivated by the imminent return of the Lord Jesus Christ; they had a sense of reward.

The model church comprises **people** who are truly *saved* —in the Lord Jesus Christ; *surrendered* to Christlikeness; *suffering* for the sake of the Lord Jesus Christ; *soul-winning,* echoing forth the truth; and living in the light of the **second coming** of Christ.

This is the church—the people—that Christ would have us be, too.

In the second chapter of 1 Thessalonians, Paul uses himself as the example to describe the ideal pastor, Christian worker, evangelist or missionary, who is to be:

—a faithful steward of the word of God, preaching the gospel;
—like a gentle mother, who nourishes and loves the church.

And like a concerned father, he:
—preached and set an example by his life, encouraged them, and was prepared to suffer for them;
—brought them comfort and consolation;
—and was never a burden to them.

Like a loving brother, he sincerely wanted to be a part of them and with them. They were truly his brethren in Christ.

I suppose that you could sum it by saying this church was a contagious church. The preaching had been authentic; there were no flattering words; there was no cloak of covetousness, and there was no seeking after self glory. Does this adequately describe our attitude to fellow believers in Christ?

The preaching and living witness of life in Christ had been a perfect example of how we should preach today. Our utterances need to be:

1. Biblical in character
2. Authentic in nature
3. Gracious in attitude
4. Relevant in approach

The expression **single–minded** comes to mind, and we need to be single-minded in the Lord's service, not double-minded! Every Christian is intended by God to live in obedience to the great commission to 'go into all the world' — and the world, of course, includes wherever you may be (workplace, the supermarket, old folks' home, local school or wherever). So the example of the church in Thessalonica is clearly for us, to challenge and encourage us to see our lives in that light, imitating the Lord, following good biblical examples of gospel living and action, and becoming an example to others.

In chapter three, the key motif is the vital need to be **established**. There is so much wavering in our own times that we need to be challenged afresh concerning this.

All new Christians go through times of testing and affliction and unless they are established and learn to **stand firm** in the Lord, they will be seriously knocked about by the devil. But remember that the devil never kicks a dead donkey!

Paul was not satisfied with just having these people saved and nurtured, he wanted to see them established and standing firm in their faith. After all, no child walks before he or she first learns to stand firm. So what means did Paul use to establish these new believers in the faith? Consider the opening verses of chapter three.

Firstly, Paul sent Timothy, his 'brother and minister of God, and our fellow labourer in the gospel of Christ, to establish you and encourage you concerning your faith....' He wanted to see if they were still standing firm with the Lord, and when Timothy reported back to Paul, the things he said about the Thessalonian Christians gave Paul every reason to feel comforted.

Secondly, he wrote them a letter. Clearly, they had needed reassurance and encouragement. Paul wanted to tell them of his love for them and give them further reassurance.

Thirdly, he prayed for them. Do you remember how elsewhere in Paul's letters, he tells Christians that they are in his mind, in his heart and in his prayers? This is the character of the godly minister of the gospel.

In chapter four, we move into the second half of the letter, which deals with practical instruction for these new believers.

If the key thought in chapter three was **be established**, the key thought here is **walk**. Paul pleads with them to be obedient to the word when he writes: 'Finally, brethren, we urge and exhort you in the Lord Jesus that you should abound more and more, just as you received from us how you ought to walk and to please God....'

Christian behaviour is often compared to a walk, for several reasons:

—To walk you need life. The dead are unable to walk.

—It requires growth; a newborn baby cannot stand, never mind walk.

—It requires liberty. Somebody who is bound up cannot walk.

—It demands light; nobody wants to walk in the dark.

—It cannot be hidden; a walk is usually seen by all.

Paul also describes to these believers the kind of walk they should have. There are four kinds:

1. A walk in holiness. (See vv. 1 – 8).
2. A walk in love. (See vv. 9 – 10).
3. A walk in honesty. (See vv. 11 – 12).
4. A walk in hope. (See vv. 13 – 18).

So let us start with the **walk in holiness**. Here, Paul essentially deals with marriage and the home. The Christian has the responsibility of building a Christian home that will glorify God, so Paul begins at this point.

Immorality can be likened to selfishness and robbery. Thus Paul encourages them to live to please God and not themselves. He had set the example (2:4), and now he expected them to follow. He had commanded them (from the Lord) to live in holiness and purity by the power of God. God's will for their lives was that they be set apart for a purpose. The word **sanctified** sums this up aptly.

Then there was the **walk in love**. Love is one of the key marks of a believer. Remember, 'Behold how they love one another', was one of the ways in which witnesses described the fellowships of the early church.

Next, there was the **walk of honesty**. Paul now talks about the believer's vocation and his contacts with unsaved people. One of the problems of the church in Thessalonica was that some of the believers had misunderstood the promise of Christ's return, given up working altogether and become parasites, living off other believers. Work, of course, is an act of spiritual worship. The Christian who does an honest day's work and who is careful to maintain a good testimony WILL influence the unsaved.

Finally, there was the **walk of hope**. To me, this is a classic passage because, as the Lord's people, we have a glorious hope: the promise of heaven; an eternity with our Lord and Saviour. Unbelievers have no real hope; their destiny is hell!

Now let us move to chapter five, the final portion of the epistle, and what is mainly a series of warnings, instructing these relatively young believers on how to live in the light of Christ's coming. We can breathe a sigh of relief here. When I read of the wonderful witness of these Thessalonian believers, it is a source of encouragement to me to know that they had to deal with a few problems and needed a little direction from their apostolic founder. I suspect that some were starting to live a little carelessly, not respecting church leadership; perhaps some were abusing the public meetings, and there was a general need for love and harmony among the saints.

These warnings are good for you and me, too. They show us how to live in harmony and peace. Paul makes six vital points:

1. **Be watchful.** (vv. 1 – 11).

Paul reminds the believers that they are children of light and they are not to walk in the darkness that had marked their former, unredeemed lives. The message is: live in the expectancy of the Lord's imminent return —this is a real motivator!

2. **Be respectful to your leaders.** (vv. 12 – 13).

Leaders in the church, and for that matter those who undertake the responsibility of leadership within workplace Christian fellowship groups, have an onerous task before them, so respect and support them in this duty. They are ultimately accountable for their actions before the Lord.

3. **Be mindful of one another.** (vv. 14 – 15).

The visible witness of a Christian says much to the world at large about the value of the gospel. If you see your brother or sister in Christ acting in an irresponsible way, you should warn them that they are bringing Christ and the church or fellowship into disrepute. Similarly, be quick to comfort and reassure those who are discouraged or feeling downhearted.

4. **Be thankful.** (vv. 16 – 18).

We live in a world that expects everything and gives nothing. We should be seen both as those who are grateful to the Lord for what he has done for us, and as warm and thankful people in all areas of life. Our witness is wonderfully reinforced, because our attitude is right.

5. **Be careful in worship.** (vv. 19 – 20).

Many Christians, in their own minds, are confused about the work of God the Holy Spirit, but he is the source of our strength and light and life. We must see him as the enabler, and as the source of our empowerment in every aspect of our lives, especially in our worship. It is he who points us to Jesus, our Saviour. But freedom in the Holy Spirit does not give us licence to behave in a manner that is disorderly or unworthy before God.

6. **Be faithful in daily conduct.** (vv. 22 – 28).

Our daily conduct is our visible witness to the world. There must not even be an appearance of evil in our lives, actions and attitudes, nor in the words we speak. Many Christians, especially at work, seem to think that they can live by a dual standard, but it is essential that in the workplace, where our colleagues see us in every condition of life, as elsewhere, we maintain a blameless manner of living. Otherwise we will be seen as hypocrites and bigots, and bring the name of our Lord and Saviour into disrepute.

In the passage that we have just looked at, we find three bold commands, which we are to obey. Obedience at this point is essential to our witness and work as disciples:

Rejoice always!
Pray without ceasing.
In everything give thanks.

The Christian who walks with the Lord, and keeps in constant communion (fellowship) with him, will see many reasons for rejoicing and thanksgiving; if your life is full of misery and boredom, then you need look no further than **yourself** to see what needs to change, and to **Jesus** to see the one who can change you!

To pray without ceasing is not to be exhibitionist! Others may not be directly aware that we are constantly in touch with the Lord in our (probably mainly silent) communion with him as we go about our daily activities. Even when we are reviewing spreadsheets, in conferences or serving customers, we can at a very deep level be conscious that we are a temple of the Holy Spirit; that Jesus dwells in us, and we in him. Often that will lead to a specific intercession in our hearts for a colleague, or an inward prayer for a word or wisdom from the Holy Spirit about an issue, situation or person. There may also be opportunities to pray openly for others. Don Latham has described the way in which colleagues in desperate personal need, sickness and distress sometimes asked him for prayer in the workplace, and were helped greatly when he then prayed (aloud) for them, with their consent.[1] We see from his accounts of such incidents that we have to be both very sensitive to God's leading in these matters and bold to obey and pray when it is right, and really desired by the colleague.

When your heart's desire is what God wills, then you are in 'prayer fellowship' with him, because the Spirit is witnessing to your spirit. Always remember that Jesus, our great high priest, is interceding for us and in us, and drawing us close to the Father.

So the formula for a closer walk with the Lord is this: remain in a continual state of fellowship and communion with the Lord, worshipping him inwardly, listening to his voice and speaking to him, throughout each day —whatever you are doing, because your life in him is constant and he is continually at work in you; live in peace and brotherly love in your fellowship; and feed on the word of God daily and systematically. (Remember that, rather as when we are on a course of antibiotics we know that the medicine will not work properly unless we continue as prescribed, so we have to be constant and faithful in Scripture reading. Unlike the antibiotics, of course, we are to continue feeding on God's word for the whole of life!) This 'course of treatment' helps us to persevere, walking in love, faith, hope and obedience. As we go on being filled with the Spirit and nourished by the Scriptures, our lives are sanctified, and we begin to grow in our walk of effective discipleship, living in the light of the imminent return of Jesus.

What a remarkable church at Thessalonica! And what a vision Paul holds up for their edification and ours. The active, effective Christian disciple is to be: Saved – Surrendered – Soul winning – Single–minded – Standing firm – Sanctified – Submitting – and aware of the Second Coming. This vision for the journey will help us to fulfil the purpose that God has preordained for each of us!

---

[1] See *Being Unmistakably Christian at Work*, Terra Nova

5

REVIVAL BEGINS AT HOME
—A STUDY IN CHOICES

A LOOK AT THE LIFE OF JOSIAH

WHAT DO WE KNOW ABOUT JOSIAH?

Josiah,[1] whose name means 'the Lord supports' was the son of the wicked king Amon. He was only eight years old when he became king. Even at that tender age, Josiah displayed godly qualities. We learn that when he was sixteen he sought the God of David. He was brought up in a time of turmoil, trouble and greed in the land of Judah. We can take it that his mother's influence was instrumental in nurturing his devotion to the Lord. Her name was Jedida (which means 'beloved of God'). Josiah represented the final flash of Judah's departing glory. His was the sunset reign!

We are going to consider briefly the implications for us of the account of the 'lost book' that was found in Josiah's reign. This is a true story about Josiah, a study in choices, which has a tremendous significance for us. When we read through the books of Kings and Chronicles we find that they tell a great story of choices —the choices made by those who were in power over the divided nations of Israel and Judah, and the choices made by the people whom they ruled.

---

[1] See 2 Kings 22–23

JOSIAH CHOSE TO FOLLOW GOD!

What can we learn from his life and deeds? Above all, Josiah chose to follow God. His *choice* was to bring about national repentance and restoration. He had a plan:

1. To **repair** the temple;
2. To **restore** worship;
3. To **rid the nation** of idols and altars.

In those days, the nation's special place for the worship of Almighty God was the temple. Today, as Christians, we have the privilege of being able to worship God wherever we are, for we are the temple of the Holy Spirit. But some pitfalls are still the same today as was the case all those centuries ago. There are things which can distract our attention from God, and which can become idols in our lives.

Something truly wonderful and awesome happened in the reign of Josiah. During the first stage of the restoration of the temple, they recovered the Book of the Law, which we must presume was carefully hidden away during the reign of one of the evil kings of Judah. This resulted in the extension to Josiah's plan for the nation, which now included:

4. The **renewal** of the Covenant
5. The **repentance** of the nation
6. The **restoration** of the Passover
7. The **revival** of a nation

The reading of the newly discovered book had a life changing impact on the lives of many. They began to realize what the attitude of God was to the way they were conducting themselves as a nation, and the result was that the nation was spiritually revived.

WHAT ABOUT US?

Is our world much different? Human nature is still as it was. The world is still so full of violence, corruption, selfishness and ungodliness. Josiah boldly challenged an apathetic, ungodly nation, and we must be prepared to do the same.

When it comes to restoring Christian values in our nation, I would reiterate the truth that apathy is the great enemy. When you consider the number of believing Christians in Britain—perhaps 350,000 out of a full time workforce of 11.3 million people—you might wonder why Christian witness in our land is not more effective. However, a number of factors seem to stand in the way of Christians making a greater impact:

- Fear of other people's responses and reactions;
- Fear of rejection and rebuttal;
- At work, a fear of management response;
- Fear of our peers;
- A lack of interest in evangelism;
- A lack of concern for others...

—in fact, utter selfishness!

I do not think any of us is completely exempt from at least an occasional temptation toward apathy. Dorothy L. Sayers reminded us of the strangeness of the fact that many who would be horrified at a pet cat killing a bird can hear, over and over again, the account of Jesus being put to death — without experiencing any sense of shock. She was writing about Christians, and about our self–centred attitude toward the atoning death of our Saviour. She had a powerful point, in that the reality of the crucifixion is often ignored.

The unconditional love of God for all of us should provide the motivation and the challenge for a different attitude. As the apostle Paul puts it: 'But God demonstrates His own love towards us, in that while we were still sinners, Christ died for us' (Romans 5:8). We should be living in constant awareness and thankfulness that Jesus made the sacrifice for our sins, that we might have eternal life with him, and be assured of the forgiveness of all our sins. He paid with his precious blood. How can we remain apathetic for an instant when we think of that amazing gift?

REPAIR THE TEMPLE!

So what motivates you? What are your waking thoughts? We need to remember the relationship that we have with God. When we 'repair the temple' — that is, when we cleanse ourselves, and get rid of those things that take our eyes off the Lord Jesus Christ — we will see real things happening, both in our own lives and in those of other people. But, at the end of the day … *It's Your Choice!*

It is time to renew your commitment to the covenant God has made with his people—including you!

If we are going to renew our covenant with God, a number of questions need to be asked and answered....

- ■ Even the very finest fruit trees need to be pruned to enable all of the growing energy to be focused into producing fine fruit.
  What are the barriers and hindrances in your life — which areas need a little pruning?
- ■ What is your dream? Do you have a vision?
  Do you ask God to give you a vision for the work that he has prepared for you, or do you find it easier just to sit and watch along the route?
- ■ At work we are often sent away on courses to encourage us to value our jobs and to embrace and take ownership of the company or organization's ethos. But what about God? —do we take ownership of his will for our lives? What value do you place on your walk with God?
- ■ Some years ago, when I was much younger and was often absorbed by my work to the exclusion of everything and everybody else, my wife would bring me back down to earth by simply asking this question: 'Just where do I figure in your list of priorities today?' An important question, no doubt, but even more important is this one: where is God in your schedule for today? Quite simply, what are your life priorities?
- ■ How do you feel about eternity? Where is Jesus, the

Saviour and Lord, in your life? Do his requirements of you sometimes seem to be a bit of an inconvenience? Do you include God in *every* aspect of life, or only in the areas where you want him to be? Do you go to places (and look at things) that you know would not please him? Or have you surrendered every facet of your life to him? Do you remember the price Jesus paid for you, and use your time for his glory?

Answer those questions honestly, for yourself. Then get your priorities right! Just because the world is in a state of moral decline and decay, this does not mean that we have to travel the same route. Josiah saw a wonderful opportunity to restore a troubled nation, and to bring peace to a people who had known no peace. He was a young man with a purpose, and we too have a similar opportunity to make a difference, to make an impact for the kingdom of God; but it depends upon you and me —our willingness to obey the word and the Spirit, and to make the right *choices* about how we are going to live our lives from now on. We can continue to live in apathy and drift ever further from the 'first love' for Jesus which came when we were born again, or we can repent and enjoy the new start that God loves to give; walking in his ways with renewed zeal and commitment.

RESTORE WORSHIP!

How can we do this? There are three simple, but yet necessary things to do, which we often neglect. But firstly, we must avoid the tyranny of the *urgent* —and, instead, dwell on the *important*. Our lives can become so preoccupied with the urgent but often unimportant things that we neglect that which is the most important of all, namely our relationship with God!

Here are three key statements from the word of God which we need to take to heart. The references to men and brethren apply similarly to women and sisters.

On Supplication Prayer

'The effective, fervent prayer of a righteous man avails much' (James 5:16). If we pray fervently, we can begin to see God's power at work in unexpected places.

On Submission to the Will of God

'I beseech you therefore, brethren, by the mercies of God, that you present your bodies a living sacrifice, holy, acceptable to God, which is your reasonable service' (Romans 12:1).

Since Jesus died for us that we might have life, then it is only reasonable that we should offer ourselves to God, for his service. He gave his life for our lives, so we are his. This should remove all self–seeking, and lead us to willing submission to his perfect will for us.

On Surrender to be like Jesus

'Let each of you look out not only for his own interests, but also for the interests of others. Let this mind be in you which was also in Christ Jesus' (Philippians 2:4–5).

This is the hard bit! But what a source of joy it is that we can indeed have the 'mind of Christ' when we know his words and obey them, hear his voice, and keep in step with the Spirit.

Above all, we need to be worshipping God in our own hearts —not only when with other believers, but every day, whatever our circumstances, wherever we are. To declare God's supreme glory, honour and majesty puts other things in their right (subordinate) places.

So where are you on the road? Where are you on the journey, in your spiritual life, today? Are you really communicating with God in a meaningful way? Are you really submitting to the will of God? Are you really surrendered —to be more like the Lord Jesus Christ? Those are very direct, personal questions. Again, they are for you to answer for yourself. Whatever your answers, be assured that God has more for you: more to give you; more of his own Spirit with which to fill, power and equip you.

There are no spiritual 'quick fixes' for you and me. God performed the mightiest miracle when he sent his Son. God became Man that he might draw us to himself, be an example to us, save us, and die for us.

READ THE BOOK!

Like Josiah, we have 'found the book', so let us read it and take it to heart. But do you have confidence in the word of God, the Bible? Paul tells us that, 'All Scripture is given by inspiration of God, and is profitable for doctrine, for reproof, for correction, for instruction in righteousness, that the man of God may be complete, thoroughly equipped for every good work' (2 Timothy 3:16). We cannot be effective in our witness if we are not familiar with the book, and known as the people of the book.

GO ON BEING FILLED WITH THE HOLY SPIRIT!

Do we have confidence in the work of the Holy Spirit in our lives —that he will fill us, renew us and empower us? Despite there being some different emphases amongst Christians concerning certain aspects of the work of the Holy Spirit, we can all agree that he is truly divine; in him we see the love and power of the godhead at work. He gives life. Jesus himself said, "And I will pray the Father, and He will give you another Helper, that He may abide with you forever—the Spirit of truth, whom the world cannot receive, because it neither sees Him nor knows Him; but you know Him, for He dwells with you and will be in you. I will not leave you orphans; I will come to you" (John 14:16 –18).

BE CONFIDENT IN PRAYER!

"We have access by faith into this grace", Paul told the church in Rome. (See Romans 5:2.) We can come into the presence of God at any time, through the gracious work of the Lord Jesus Christ —but do we use that privilege?

REPENT!

The result of reading the Book of the Law was repentance. What does 'repentance' mean? It is, of course, both turning *away* from what is wrong and turning *to* God, depending only on divine grace for forgiveness. It includes sorrow that we have offended God and broken his perfect law, and a desire to return to the way of obedience. To repent is a decision — an act of the will, made possible by grace. The marks of true repentance include re-evaluating our lives—our thoughts, actions and words—and changing for the better in those areas where we have been falling short of God's pattern, or straying into disobedience. A sense of regretfulness might begin to help spur us on to such a change of heart and direction, but such a feeling is certainly not enough. For real change to ensue there must be that turning of the whole person from sin to God.

When Josiah had the Book of the Law read out to him, he heard how it revealed God's anger; it was made clear that God was a God of justice and wrath against sin and disobedience. As a consequence, he repented; he enquired of the Lord's will, and then had the book read before the people and their leaders.

Repentance means a separation from those things that would distract us from the Lord! Paul said to the Thessalonians, "You turned to God from idols, to serve the true and living God." Remember where Thessalonica was located, effectively at the foot of Mount Olympus, the home of the false gods of Greek religion. The turning from idolatry of those to whom Paul was writing had been true repentance. This made news! But it did not happen by accident. The word of God had to be preached, and a response of faith prompted by the Holy Spirit. There had to be repentance. You have everything given to you to use to live a glorious life for God, but... *It's Your Choice!*

OUR RESPONSE

Remember that always, in all situations, whether at home or in the workplace, we are called to share the love of God. In New Testament Greek, there are several different words which are translated into the single English word 'love'. In the original language, the love that Christ commands us to share is not these:

Eros – the sensual and passionate;
Philia – love for your nearest and dearest;
Storge – the parent and child affection.

No. Rather, the love of Christ is 'agape'. 'Agape' love is a 'living', unselfish love that does not envy, does not parade itself, is not puffed up, does not behave rudely, does not seek its own, is not provoked, thinks no evil, does not rejoice in sin, but rejoices in truth, bears all things, believes all things, hopes all things and endures all things – *and this love never fails.*

WHAT WAS JOSIAH'S RESPONSE?

Josiah looked at the book and what he saw was God's righteous nature. He knew that God would be angry! We look at the cross, and we see the cost of sin, mercy and grace! Josiah saw what the price of sin was: separation from God. Justice would require that we should pay the price for our sin —but Christ paid it for us, and we receive that amazing free gift by grace, through faith in him.

Here is what happened in the reign of Josiah, and what can happen in our own lives....

- The book was recovered.
  We can restore the place of the Bible in our own lives.
- The people repented, and they confessed to God.
  We can confess our own sins to the Lord.
- The temple, the place of worship, was repaired.
  We can repair the place of worship in our own hearts.
- The nation was reformed. The idols were cleared out of Judah.
  We can remove our own false gods and receive new life.
- The nation was restored. Worship of God was put back into the temple.
  God can be present in our hearts and lives.
- Judah was revived.
  Our own nation will never be revived until we are revived.

BEWARE THE DEVIL!

Paul wrote to Timothy about 'itching ears', and we can suffer from a similar syndrome today. I suspect that we would not have so many denominations (and so many different, false religions) if, as a people, we were not always looking for 'something different'. But remember: the first attack of Satan was a questioning of the word God had spoken —seeking to change the human perception of it, so that divine revelation would come to be thought of by many as inadequately expressing God's perfect will. But God's revealed word is truth, which stands for ever. So protect your mind! It is the battleground. God speaks to you in his word. Listen to him! So Eve began to doubt the word and to distort the truth; Adam, for his part, was no better. As a result, mankind has been reaping the effects of disobedience ever since.

Protect your relationships at home as well as at work from the attacks of the enemy. Remember to preserve the following, all of which are part of your Christian witness:

- Your personal purity;
- Your purity of heart, mind and motives;
- Your purity of habits;
- Your visible witness.

If we are really seeking to live for Christ, especially in the workplace, we are part of two 'congregations' —the congregation where we worship every Sunday morning, and the weekday 'congregation', whose members are often waiting to call us bigots and hypocrites when we do not live out our faith. They are not our enemies. Jesus died for them. Our real enemy is Satan. But we are not helpless, nor defenceless. We can put on our spiritual armour daily. The word of God as we take it into ourselves, feeding on it, and the Spirit of God, as we go on being filled and open to his work in us, keep us in a place of peace with God. Nothing and no-one can take that away from us, no matter what circumstances and opposition we face each day.

Satan cannot take away your salvation, but he can remove you from witness and spoil your life—if you let him; if you fail to resist him. Resist the enemy and he will flee!

How are we going to make a difference and use the opportunities that come our way—not by 'chance' but by divine appointment? By returning again and again to a clear focus on our chief purpose in life: to glorify God in all that we do. So...

- Be confident in the power of God's precious word. It is the power of God unto salvation.
- Be confident about prayer. We should 'Pray Until Something Happens' (P.U.S.H) ! Keep praying!
- Be confident in the work and power of the Holy Spirit.
- Be loving. To show love is to reveal and share God's greatest gift to us.
- Be vigilant. Satan is real and he will not like what you are doing, so do not give him a beachhead.

Remember the exciting truth that the gospel is infinitely more powerful than the work of the enemy. Revival, restoration and repentance can come to our land, but repentance in the household of God—turning from our liberal and unholy ways, our doubt, fear and unbelief—is a vital prerequisite to playing our part as effective witnesses and workers in God's kingdom. We need to allow God to work revival in us, in our hearts and minds, so that we are living in *constant* personal revival, no matter what is going on in society, in the world around us. We are to rid ourselves of those things which distract us from God; renewing our hearts and minds daily through our openness to the work of the Holy Spirit in us; reading the word of God and allowing him to speak to us through it —daily; and becoming prayer warriors and realising the power of prayer —again, daily!

The apostle Paul wrote this to the church at Philippi: 'The things that you have learned and received and heard and saw in me, these do and the God of peace will be with you.' He leaves it to them to make the choice to do that —or not to. Simple obedient faith brings glory to God, but remember: it is a choice, and one only you can make.

To conclude this section, let us recall the reasons why God became man and walked this earth. Although God is high and lifted up, he came all the way from heaven's glory to fallen mankind, in order to destroy the devil's work, and to bring blessings for all of us: to undo the damage done by the disobedience of Adam, Eve and the whole human race, offering to us restoration of the divine image in which we were made but which has been so disfigured by sin. We are all in need of what only he can give. No longer is he far away from us, where we cannot touch him or see him; he is truly 'Immanuel' —God with us.

I am reminded of the moving story, which is sometimes told, of the young American soldier serving in Germany, who at the end of the Second World War met and married a young German girl. Life was sweet until, one day in 1947, his unit was sent back to the United States. Because of the laws prevailing at that time, he was not allowed to bring his wife back with him. For over two years this young man fought the red tape of bureaucracy, and after a two and a half year battle the rules were changed and she was allowed to set sail for the USA. The young soldier greeted his lovely young wife in one of the finest embraces ever, as she—who was also his lover and best friend—was returned to him! When I think of that story, it reminds me that God is *our* great lover! He loved us infinitely more than any human being could do; he wrote his love letters in the Bible; he showed us his glory on the land, sea and in the heavens; he spoke to mankind through the patriarchs, through men and women of faith who heard his voice: he spoke through the Law and the prophets. But, from the perspective of sinful and disobedient man, he often still seemed distant. Finally, when Jesus Christ came down to earth, we were enabled to rejoice fully, with a joy unspeakable, because at last God was very near —with us in our humanity.

We read that, 'the Word became flesh and dwelt among

us.' God 'tabernacled' with us —the Jews could understand that because, as their forefathers wandered through the wilderness to the promised land, God's presence was made known in a special way in a tabernacle. Now we know in a much more personal way that, as we journey through life, we are NOT alone! He came to dwell among us —to live with us! Jesus, God's only begotten Son, lived with his people in the flesh for thirty three years; now he lives with us through his Spirit! Indeed, when we believe and receive Jesus as Lord and Saviour, in accordance with his promise, he dwells in us and we in him. John, who had written the words 'we beheld his glory' still knew, even in his old age, that there was no mistake about it all, for he had seen Jesus for himself, known his friendship during the Lord's earthly ministry and in a new way after the resurrection.

What can we say of those who met Jesus in the flesh? What glory they beheld! They saw the glory of a perfect life; the glory of his mighty deeds; they heard the glory in his speech. They beheld the glory of his transfiguration; the glory of his resurrection, and the glory of his ascension — they saw it all. John saw that it was the glory of God shining in Jesus; that he was the only begotten Son of the Father, full of grace and truth.

When God became man, it was revealed clearly that he understands our problems and sympathises with our sorrows. Of course he always did: he is omniscient; he never changes. But now the truth was manifested in human form. God could have sent his Son to earth fully grown! But instead he was born of a woman and brought up as a normal child. What an awesome truth, which should fill us with hope.

He became a man to set an example for us. If Jesus had not been who he was, but an angel instead, we could never have copied him, but he became a man, setting an example for us —that we should follow in his footsteps. All that is noble and strong in a man, all that is graceful and tender in a woman, all that is winsome and engaging in children, indeed all that is lovely in anyone, is found in Jesus Christ, and we should try to be like him. We cannot be like him if we let sin reign over us. We cannot be like him if we are selfish, mean, hateful and worldly. Oh, I do know that we will never be *just* like him, but that should not stop us from trying to be *more* like him. Yes, he became a man in order to set an example for us.

Finally, above all, he became a man so that he could die in our place. This is the main reason why Jesus came to earth to dwell with and amongst us. He was wounded for our transgressions.... It is a wonderful thing to contemplate: that he came to draw us to the Father, so that we may enjoy his presence for all eternity; it is a wonderful thing that he came to take on our humanity and experience, as one of us, our frailty and needs. It is a wonderful thing that he came to be an example for us. But all of these things would have been meaningless if he had not come to die for us poor lost, hell-bound sinners.

You may have seen some spectacular sights in this world: mountains, lakes, forests, rivers and seas; the sunrises and the sunsets. But your greatest vision will be when you look up from your sins and see the Lord Jesus Christ dying slowly and painfully on a cross to save you from those sins. I am so glad that I saw him and that he found me. Are you?

Yes, that is the amazing reality which we are to keep constantly at the forefront of our minds both at work and at home: that the Word became flesh. God became man, the most wonderful and perfect one, because he loved us, and still loves us, with a perfect love.

God is indeed a great mystery to this world, and his coming here as a man is a mystery to many. I like the story about the first time the cosmonauts went into space and it all seemed rather primitive; then, as they came before the cameras of the world's media, thumbs under their braces, looking so proud of their achievement, one of them said, 'We've been in the air, we've been round the earth and we did not see God.'

The following Sunday, W.A. Criswell, the eminent Bible commentator, made a classic remark, 'Ah, they may well boast, but if they had stepped out of their space suits, they surely would have met God.'

Well, the world *has* seen God, and can still see him at work in the world, because the Lord Jesus Christ came to earth and dwelt amongst us. The word became flesh and dwelt among us —because he loved you and me, and he was willing to suffer for us, that you and I might live in, for and to him for all eternity. When we truly keep these revealed truths in our hearts and minds, we will be able to allow the Holy Spirit to soften our hearts, dissolving our apathy as we long, once again, to be at the heart of a work of revival, telling others of this amazing good news. Are you beginning to gain a vision and a desire to offer to those alongside whom you work each day what you yourself have been so freely given?

6

CLIMBING IN THE LAND OF SHALLOW GRAVES

Traditionally, in times of warfare, shallow graves were used for the temporary burial of the dead. That provides an apt picture of the sad condition in which many Christians who have succumbed to apathy find themselves. Apathy is a desperately serious pitfall, and when a Christian falls into such a pit, he discovers that it has sides which are so steep that it seems almost impossible to climb out! The problem is so often that we may have travelled in the same way on the same route for a long time, and in the process have lost sight of why we are on it —and we may not have kept our eyes focussed on Jesus. In so many ways, he warned his disciples of the problems that can arise on the path of faith, and this study would be wholly unrealistic if we did not address this area.

We may simply have become too comfortable with the way things are, the familiar routines and the predictable round; and there may well be fears about the unknown, gradually hardening us against the call to more radical discipleship. But if you spend some time reading about the lives of those Christians who have really stepped out in faith, you will be greatly encouraged to do battle against apathy.

What is it that keeps us from climbing out of the rut?

Selfishness! When we begin to hear a fresh call of God to a deeper level of discipleship or worship, a fresh move of obedience, or some new area of mission at home, work or farther afield, our minds so often react: 'but what about *me*?' How will I cope? Will this bring me pleasure or pain? What is *my* desire in this matter? Selfishness is sin. Self-absorption and excessive self-interest can indicate a lack of trust in God and a faithlessness that ignores all that Christ has done for us.

In chapter two of Paul's letter to the Ephesians, he explains how sin always works against us. Before salvation, we were dead in our sin and trespasses, without hope. We were disobedient, walking in the ways of the world, the flesh and the devil. In the letter to the Romans he wrote graphically of the depravity of unregenerate man, motivated mainly by the lusts of the flesh. The reality of a lost eternity facing those who do not repent is made absolutely clear throughout the New Testament.

When we came to Christ, personally receiving him as Saviour and Lord, we were given a new life. God then gave us a fresh start. All our sins were forgiven, and I suppose we could say that we are redeemed for a second opportunity at life, but this time with the power of God available to us; now the power that raised Jesus from the dead is at work in us for we are a new creation. Here is the heart of the matter. Here is the scriptural key that will lift us out of the 'shallow grave' which awaits the apathetic. Here is the truth which will enable us to keep moving in continuous personal revival.

We turn first to Romans, chapter six, where Paul sets out some clear guidelines for the new Christian, things to which mature Christians need to return from time to time, especially when we feel apathy creeping in! He sets out clearly three things that we should know (my emphasis, in each case):

...Or do you not **know** that as many of us as were baptized into Christ Jesus were baptized into His death? (v. 3).

When we came to faith in Christ, our old self was put to death. Everything in us which is opposed to God is to be 'crucified' or put to death. We live a new life in Jesus, who died for us. We need to be living in constant awareness of this vital truth! How can we be complacent or apathetic when we have this tremendous scriptural assurance that we are in him and he is in us; that the benefits of his precious death are ours as his free gift?

...**knowing** this, that our old man was crucified with Him, that the body of sin might be done away with, that we should no longer be slaves of sin. (v. 6).

So we believe and fully acknowledge that Christ went to the cross to pay the price for our sin, that our sins were 'nailed to the cross', that we might no long be controlled by our sinful nature. Instead, we are to keep in step with the Holy Spirit, whose temple we are. If we really are open to the continual in–filling of the Spirit, we will not lapse into apathy!

...**knowing** that Christ, having been raised from the dead, dies no more. Death no longer has dominion over Him. (v. 9).

Christ died once, to deal with our sin, that we might have eternal life. Death no longer has the last word! Our true, sure hope is for eternity in the presence of our Lord. Nothing can take that hope from us. Mindful of it, we cannot be apathetic. We want others to know the truth!

The old nature—the way of death, which used to rule our hearts—no longer has any authority over us.

Paul then tells us to **reckon** these three statements together,

Likewise you also, **reckon** yourselves to be dead indeed to sin, but alive to God in Christ Jesus our Lord. Therefore do not let sin reign in your mortal body, that you should obey it in its lusts. (vv. 11 & 12).

These statements, reckoned together, deliver a powerful message to our hearts: they are both a reminder of the new standing we have been given by grace, through the perfect sacrifice of Jesus Christ, and also the greatest incentive to repent of any apathetic tendency our self–examination reveals!

In verses 13 and 19 we are told to yield ourselves to God, as those who are now 'alive from the dead', giving our bodies to him, as instruments of righteousness, and that we are told to be 'slaves of righteousness for holiness'.

If we take these verses to heart, make them our own and begin to walk in renewed obedience to the commands which they contain, we can enjoy so many benefits:

- Assurance as to the past, that all our sins have been dealt with;
- Assurance as to the present, that God will work in us and through us, for good;
- Assurance as to the future: affliction cannot destroy us, and our eternity is secure in Christ.
- This assurance is guaranteed and confirmed to us by God's manifest love toward us in Christ

The New Testament constantly encourages Christians to look at the abundant blessings that are ours. We have already been blessed, '...with every spiritual blessing in the heavenly places in Christ'. (See Ephesians 1:3). Look at the Lord's many wonderful promises, and especially those in John 10:28–29, '...neither shall anyone snatch them out of My hand', and '...no-one is able to snatch them out of My Father's hand.' Look what God has done us —the Father sent the Son to be the Saviour of the world; your Saviour and mine! Knowing these things, climb out of the rut of selfishness, the 'shallow grave', and follow him with renewed zeal.

God has mapped out a purpose for our lives:

For we are His workmanship, created in Christ Jesus for good works, which God prepared beforehand that we should walk in them.

Ephesians 2:10

God has plans and purposes for all of us, but it has to be said that many people are not in the places where they are supposed to be, so are neither fulfilling God's best purposes nor enjoying all the blessings he has for them. To 'predestine' is to determine something beforehand. God has ordained for your future what he determined you are on earth to do. It is the inner purpose for your life. It is the real reason for breathing. There is a condition which has been pre-ordained by God just for you.

Solomon wrote, 'I have seen servants on horses, while princes walk on the ground like servants.' (See Ecclesiastes 10:7). In this verse we read of one who had been pre–ordained to be a prince yet who nonetheless walked as a servant. Walking in servanthood is precisely what we have been called to do, even as we rejoice in the standing Jesus won for us, his free gift to those who receive him. Our calling, God's purpose for us, is certainly not to lie around in the 'valley of the shallow graves'.

God's specific plan for you is what is written in heavenly records concerning you. It was the original intention of God, even before he created you.

Is life nothing more than education, marriage, children, holidays, money, work, retirement, and then death? Of course not! Such matters have their proper place, but they are not to be our prime motivation. Underlying everything is our relationship with the Lord.

Wherever we are on our journey through life, we need to be aware that spiritual mishaps sometimes occur and confuse men. The evil 'prince of the air', Satan, laughs men to scorn, knowing that we are not where we are supposed to be. We need to be acquainted with the weapons we are to use in our battle against a determined enemy who tries to snatch away from us our awareness of God's purpose for our lives. His activity is sometimes rather like that of a vulture. The vulture is a large bird of prey which does not seize or tear its food, nor does it kill other animals. Rather, it feeds on the dead flesh of creatures which have been killed or have died naturally. They are birds a lot of people do not want to see. The vulture is ugly: most of its head and neck is featherless. Vultures can smell death. There is something planted in them that lets them know when death is imminent. In a war, one of the ugliest sights must be of a soldier who is wounded, and is fighting for his last breath, whilst a vulture waits patiently for the onset of death. They have acute sight and a sharp sense of smell. The very real truth is that there are thousands of 'spiritual vultures' waiting to feed, or already feeding, on our spiritual destinies.

There are more people living on earth now than ever before, and change in so many areas has become extremely rapid. Information is stored, processed and transmitted with amazing efficiency. Globalisation has become the norm in many areas of economic activity. For some people that has brought a massively higher standard of living; for others it has had very different results. But whatever all this change means to you, whatever your material wealth or poverty, the spiritual vulture can still attack. The 'vulture' that consumed the destiny of Esau consisted of an ordinary bowl of food. The 'destiny vulture' of some people takes the form of an over–dependence on comfort; for others, it comes through a lack of patience or unwillingness to persevere. For others, the vulture appears in the form of deception of some kind. This is a vital warning message. Destiny vultures of many kinds are in operation over mankind. God, who is omniscient and omnipotent, has a destiny for you; his will, revealed in Jesus Christ, is that you should enjoy new life in all its fullness, in him. Within that eternal destiny which all Christians share, he wants you to co-operate with him and find your particular calling. The apostles had various callings and every Christian today has some particular task or tasks to which we are called. Be assured that God really does have a best plan for you —especially for you.

We should all pray the prayer of Joseph, that the Lord will show us our divine destiny. Although he was in jail between the ages of seventeen and thirty, he still fulfilled his divine destiny because the Lord had shown him what he was supposed to be.

There is nothing more tragic than to forfeit one's divine destiny. A bird with a broken wing cannot fly. It is a disaster to forfeit the reason why you came here. There is no one else who is exactly like you. Your genes and fingerprints are peculiar to you. So it is with your destiny in God's plan. When the enemy takes one away from the place of one's divine destiny, it is a disaster. When Elijah was not in his place of destiny, he prayed and the Lord did not answer. He just asked him what he was doing where he was. "Elijah, what are you doing here?" He was in a wrong place.

Do you sense that there is opposition to you as you seek to fulfil your calling? Be encouraged! Unless there is a contest, no one can win anything —and if you do not have a destiny to pursue, why are you here? Those who pursue their destiny are indeed subject to attacks. When a person is not where he is supposed to be, there can be no battle to fight and win.

Your destiny can only be fulfilled when it is intact. I am sure that there is a department in the kingdom of darkness that specialises in 'destiny manipulation'. When a person is manipulated out of the place where he should be, prayers and Bible reading become hard work for him. But that is not the end of the story. God is always willing to provide the means for a fresh start or restoration.

STRATEGIES USED BY 'DESTINY VULTURES'

The strategies of 'destiny vultures' are many, but the major one is to make a person ignorant of his personal destiny in Christ. "And you shall know the truth, and the truth shall make you free" (John 8:32). It is the truth *known* that sets us free; the truth which is not known cannot set one free. Ignorance of your destiny means that you are living without the blueprint God intends for you. Moses was one of many great biblical characters who had a blueprint and divine direction. He learnt that he needed to do everything in accordance with God's pattern. But do *you* know the blueprint of *your* destiny? That course which you studied: were you divinely instructed? If you have a wrong blueprint, the entire structure you put on the foundation collapses. If you have not already done so, it is worth asking God to show you the blueprint of your destiny now. It is not too late to do so.... Walking in line with his plan for you, you can enjoy certainty amid the storms of life. Before a house is built, there must be a plan or blueprint, and without knowing what this is you cannot build in the best way. If the plan is not known, or if it is lost, imprisoned or buried, the vultures have won a battle.

Sometimes those 'destiny vultures' would encourage people to give in to a delusion. Sometimes we see Christians succumb to some false or unbalanced line of teaching. All too easily, if we have not laid secure, biblical foundations or are not maintaining our fellowship with Jesus, this kind of pitfall appears. Apathy is one kind of danger; another is an unwillingness to do the sort of checking of directive words from others against the clear witness of Scripture. Yet another is to fall away from the life of praise and worship; another is to lose the vital priority of Christian love, becoming mechanically 'religious', rather than being filled with grace and showing compassion. Get out of the land of shallow graves! Pray that you will discover who you really are — and that you will learn more of God's best plan and purpose for you personally. Jesus asked the disciples who the world thought he was —though, of course, he knew perfectly who he was! He dwells in you and you in him, and he wants nothing less for you than that you should know who you are in him, and what he is calling you to do with the rest of your life. So do you know who you really are?

Pray that God will show you your destiny. Walk in holiness, honesty and integrity. Learn and believe the wonderful affirmations that the New Testament makes concerning you and all men and women of faith, our adoption, our inheritance with all the saints, our sonship and our eternal destiny. Take hold of those precious assurances in the word of God.

Just as the vulture is patient, destiny manipulators can wait for a person to make a mistake or fall into one of those pitfalls we have mentioned, or simply to become weary or careless —then they attack. If you do not know your standing in Christ, servants will 'take your horse', and then you, 'the prince' will be walking on the ground. It is time for the Holy Spirit to reschedule your life. It is time to know where you should really be. It is time to analyze where you are and where you are going, and to see what you need to do to get there.

UNDERSTANDING WHAT THE WILL OF THE LORD IS

So let us try to think practically about the Lord's will for our individual lives. The perfect starting point is to be found in Ephesians 5:15 –17.

See then that you walk circumspectly, not as fools but as wise, redeeming the time, because the days are evil. Therefore do not be unwise, but understand what the will of the Lord is.

There are times for all of us when we stand at the threshold of life's decisive moments, when we ask the question, "Where do I go from here?" The Epistle to the Ephesians answers such vital questions as these: Who are we? Where have we come from? What has God done for us? What does he expect of us? It is in this last section that Paul encourages the Ephesian Christians to **understand what the will of the Lord is**! For us as individual believers, as well as for the body of Christ generally, every moment of every day beckons us to understand what the will of the Lord is. Jesus indicated that he had come to do the will and work of the Father. Paul put it this way: "For it is God who works in you both to will and to do for His good pleasure" (Philippians 2:13). God has put us on this earth to do *his* will and *his* work. Therefore it is indeed imperative that we understand what the will of the Lord is. So let us consider how can we do so.

WE MUST BE SEEKING TO DO HIS WILL (v. 15a)

As we seek to be about doing God's will, I hear Paul saying two things: "See then...." and "walk circumspectly" or, as I would put it, 'look and live!'

LOOK AT YOUR OWN LIFE.
When Paul says "See...", he means take a careful look at your own desires and motives. Take close account of your own attitudes and actions. Are they in line with what you know God desires from you right now? God desires that his people be pure and holy, upright and righteous, moral and ethical. If we are not, then how can a holy God reveal his plan further?

LIVE LIFE DOING GOD'S WILL.
When Paul says "Walk...", he means conduct your life carefully. The Christians in Ephesus were living at a time when evil pressed in on them from every side. We, too, live in a society surrounded by impulses to 'do our own thing' and influences that may dissuade us from doing God's will. But all of life is intended to be lived in the light of God's revealed will and word inasmuch as we understand it.

IN UNDERSTANDING WHAT THE WILL OF THE LORD IS, WE MUST BE THINKING THROUGH HIS WILL

In Ephesians 5:15 and 17, as we have seen, Paul contrasts the foolish or thoughtless person with the one who is wise and discerning. The wise person tries to think and see life from God's perspective, which can only be revealed by the Holy Spirit. So think through God's will, and apply that knowledge to life, in these practical ways:

SPEND QUALITY TIME TALKING WITH THE LORD.

James 1:5 says, "If any of you lacks wisdom, let him ask of God, who gives to all liberally and without reproach, and it will be given to him." As we pray, God works on our wills and makes us wise to do his will. If you will allow God's thoughts to run through your reading of—and meditation on—Scripture you will be astonished at the insight God will give you in understanding his will from the word. Then the inner witness of the Holy Spirit can impress and empower you to think through and understand what God's will is. As you think through his will, check to see that what you sense in prayer, hear in Scripture and experience in your circumstances all line up in the same direction.

SHARE YOUR THOUGHTS WITH TRUSTED FRIENDS.

Friends may see things you cannot see. Their point of view will be different because of their experiences as well as their personalities. Thinking something through with a friend may help you to be more objective. Talking enables you to express how you feel, and on many occasions I have ended up seeing things more clearly in my search for the will of God simply by talking something through. Understanding what the will of the Lord is comes as we talk it out with the Lord and as we think through it with trusted Christian friends.

WE MUST BE WAITING UPON HIS WILL

Two issues concerning time are involved, when we are truly seeking to understand what the will of the Lord is.

WAITING INVOLVES *TIME*.

In Ephesians 5:16, the term 'redeeming' has an intensive meaning: to buy up; to free up; to make the most of. That is to say, use your time wisely. One of the Greek words translated 'time' is *chronos*, from which we get our word chronological, which leads us to think of minutes, hours, days, weeks, months, and years. That meaning may lead you to think of waiting as a passive, inactive mode of being. But waiting on the Lord is anything but passive! You will be praying—hopefully with a passion, watching circumstances, asking for God's perspective, and sharing with other believers, while continuing to do the last thing God told you to do. This kind of active 'waiting' is worthwhile. While you wait, use your time to the fullest possible advantage, because once it has passed, not even the wisest person can recover it.

WAITING ALSO INVOLVES *TIMING*.

The Greek word Paul uses for time here is *kairos*. This refers to a specific time, a special time. It speaks of a moment of particular opportunity. The timing of how things work out is very important in God's economy. The coming of Jesus was at just the right time for his people to receive him and be a witness to the whole world. God's will, of course, can be done any time, in any place. Yet there is a sense in which, in God's timing, there is a particular person for a particular task, and we really can know when we have been personally called to do or pursue something at God's specially chosen moment.

We have thought about the centrality of our battle against apathy in the 'land of shallow graves'. Now recall again— and take to heart—that great truth that you are indeed 'his workmanship, created in Christ Jesus for good works, which God prepared beforehand that we should walk in them.' As you go about your daily work, remember that you are not just a cog in a machine, but a beloved child of your heavenly Father; you are not just a 'consumer' of material goods, you are a producer in the kingdom of God. He made you, he loves you; he redeemed you; he has a perfect plan for you; he has many good things still lined up for you to do; he has given you his word and he pours out his Spirit to enable you to discover his will; to know it, understand it and do it. He has given you brothers and sisters in Christ to help and be helped by.... So be encouraged; be positive in what you affirm about yourself and others; be biblical in your understanding; do not be a mere passenger in the church, be creative —in his strength, and giving Jesus all the glory.

As redeemed believers, we now belong to our Lord Jesus Christ. He has not only bought us, he has also made us a new creation! What is more, he has a plan for our lives, which means we have a destiny this side of heaven. In this chapter we have seen something of the way the enemy would seek to attack us, but when we apply the word in the power of the Spirit, and use those precepts in Ephesians 5, gaining wisdom from above and learning what the Lord's will is for our lives, we see both that God is infinitely more powerful than the enemy, and also that we can have complete confidence, assurance and trust in the Father's love, and can really *know* his plan for us.

Let your prayer, and your heart's desire, be to understand what the will of the Lord is. Each of us can understand what God's will is if we really long to *do* his will, are willing to *think through* his will, and will *wait* upon his will. When we do this, we will discover with joy that our strength is renewed, our zeal for the gospel returns and apathy is banished from our lives.

7

KNOW YOUR ENEMY....

There are certain things that we need to know about our spiritual enemy. We must start by taking some assurance from two points from the Book of Job: firstly, God will not allow the devil to kill those who are his; but, secondly, he will allow us to be tested and tried!

Satan is a powerful individual —and, yes, he is an individual with a personality. His personality and his characteristics are seriously powerful. Let me outline his character.

He is a deceiver. His target is our minds, his weapons are lies, and his purpose is to try and make us *ignorant* of the will of God.

He is a destroyer. He targets our bodies, his weapon is suffering, and his purpose is to make us *impatient* with God's will.

He is the ruler or 'prince' of this world —his target is our will, his weapon pride, and his purpose is to make us *independent* of God's will.

He is the accuser, his target is our heart and conscience, his weapon is accusation, and his purpose is to challenge God's will.

We who are saved cannot lose our salvation, for God the Father, '...has delivered us from the power of darkness and conveyed us into the kingdom of the Son of His love' (Colossians 1:13).

What Satan can do, very powerfully, is to bring confusion and division, distraction and deception. He will seek to attack us where we are weakest, making big issues out of small ones. What we have to remember is that, 'He who is in you is greater than he who is in the world' (1 John 4:4).

For the one who is seeking, Satan's is the voice within that says things like 'Don't listen —I can offer you a better way than God's'; or, more subtly, 'Leave it until next week, there's no rush to respond to God's prompting today.'

What does the Bible say about the devil? Jesus tells us that he was a murderer from the beginning and does not stand in the truth, because there is no truth in him. (See John 8:44.) We read in Genesis chapter three that he is craftier than any beast of the field.

When Satan wanted to lead the first man and woman into sin, he started by an attack on the mind. The continuing relevance of this is made clear to us by Paul when he writes, 'But I fear, lest somehow, as the serpent deceived Eve by his craftiness, so your minds may be corrupted from the simplicity that is in Christ' (2 Corinthians 11:3).

Why should Satan want to attack your mind? —because we were created in the image of God, and when we become a new creation in Jesus Christ and then begin to take into our minds the word of God, the renewal of the mind becomes of key importance in making us effective Christians. God's will is that you should have the mind of Christ. The devil desires that you should not have it! God speaks to us and reveals his will to us. The renewed mind is a powerful tool in the kingdom at this point, as it becomes conformed more and more to God's revealed word and we learn to walk in obedience.

Some Christians have mistakenly minimised the importance of the mind. Our minds are a battlefield. If we leave our minds empty and unguarded, there is no saying what will come to fill them. Have nothing to do with those forms of deceptive 'meditation' which encourage emptying of the mind. Rather, fill your mind with the word of God! God will renew our lives as he renews our minds through his truth. His Spirit—the Spirit of the risen Christ—is within those who are his, to empower, and enable us to overcome. We are like Paul when he was on trial, and we can say the Lord stands with us to strengthen us. Always!

If Satan can get you to believe a lie, then he can begin to work in your life, perhaps leading you into sin. This is why he starts with the mind, and this is why we must protect our minds. How did the Lord Jesus do it when he was tempted? —No great army of angels, simply the word of God:

...man shall not live by bread alone; but man lives by every word that proceeds from the mouth of the LORD.
See Deuteronomy 8:3

You shall not tempt the LORD your God.
See Deuteronomy 6:16

You shall worship the LORD your God, and Him only you shall serve.
See Matthew 4:10

It is interesting to note that when Satan quoted the word of God to Jesus, as he tried to persuade him to throw himself down the mountain, he selected only parts of Psalm 91. Satan missed the words, 'To keep you in all your ways' and, 'You shall tread upon the lion and the cobra, the young lion and the serpent you shall trample under foot.' It was, as we will see later, a speciality of the devil, to misquote and misrepresent the word of God to those he attempts to confuse.

If it is not true, Paul writes, then do not let it enter your mind.

In recent years, science has brought to light many fascinating things about the mind. It is sometimes claimed that our minds are a bit like computers, only better! It is true that we can store millions of facts, events, impressions and emotions and then recall them years later, through our memory. We can even think about the future with our imaginations. But, as we use our minds, we need to know that how we think affects our feeling, our will, our heart. A computer has neither a mind (in the true sense) nor a spirit. It cannot have consciousness. The human mind is an amazing thing, created by God, fallen, so prone to thinking in distorted, ungodly ways; but, in the Christian, the mind is in the process of being renewed by word and Spirit. Satan knows the tremendous power of your mind, and he is trying to capture it for himself. Paul, writing to the Romans, reminds us that, 'those who live according to the flesh set their minds on the things of the flesh, but those who live according to the Spirit, the things of the Spirit. For to be carnally minded is death, but to be spiritually minded is life and peace' (8:5–6). So guard your mind!

Your mind affects your whole being, but I must disagree profoundly with exponents of what we now call 'success psychology'! The Scriptures do support the position that our *attitudes* are important to our health and success in life. If our attitudes reflect sin and rebellion against the word of God, we harm both ourselves and others.

We are not to neglect our minds, which should mean that we feed on the word of God; nor should we neglect proper attention to the body. Yes, we are body, mind and spirit, but a great insight God gives us through the Hebrew concept of personhood is that each of us is a unity. God cares for us as whole persons, and we are the temple of the Holy Spirit, so we should care appropriately for the body, taking proper exercise and eating and drinking wisely. The enemy can attack us in many ways, and one way he might do so is by leading us to believe that the proper care of our bodies is unimportant. Jesus healed people; the apostles healed people; healing takes place today when God releases it, so clearly our bodies are not insignificant to our heavenly Father!

Satan is the subtle deceiver —the serpent, remember. In the Genesis account of the first great deception, we get some idea of how to deal with him. Notice the steps that he used with Eve, to get her to believe his lie. Firstly, he questioned the word of God — 'has God said...?' He did not deny that God had spoken; he simply questioned whether God had really said what Eve thought God had said. What an attack on the mind, or power of recollection! The suggestion was planted that perhaps she had misheard or misunderstood what God had said. The devil's suggestion is that you owe it to yourself to rethink what God has commanded. It is a bit like those many people today who deny that God's laws are fixed, firm and unchangeable. The devil tried the same thing with our Lord in the wilderness.

Jesus showed us what it is to be steadfast, resisting the enemy's attacks. Satan denied God's word: 'You surely shall not die!' It is but one short step from questioning God's word to denying it altogether. Adam and Eve had never seen death; all that they had to go on was God's word, but in truth this was all that they needed —God's word! If Eve had not listened to Satan questioning God's word, she would never have fallen into the trap when he denied the word of God. Satan also said, 'You will be like God'. But Adam and Eve were already made in the image of God, and Satan tempted them with an even greater sounding privilege: to be like God. This was, of course, Satan's great ambition when he was Lucifer, God's angelic servant.

How you are fallen from heaven, O Lucifer, son of the morning! How you are cut down to the ground, you who weakened the nations! For you have said in your heart: I will ascend into heaven, I will exalt my throne above the stars of God; I will also sit on the mount of the congregation, On the farthest sides of the north; I will ascend above the heights of the clouds, I will be like the Most High.

Isaiah 14:12–14

97

Don't you want to praise and thank God for the next verse: 'Yet you shall be brought down to Sheol, to the lowest depths of the Pit.' But this is for the future!

Satan is a created being, but he wanted to be worshipped and served like the Creator. It was this attitude that led him to rebel against God and seek to establish his own kingdom. 'You will be like God' is one of the gigantic lies that has controlled civilisation since the Fall of man.

Paul taught that people had, '...exchanged the truth of God for the lie, and worshiped and served the creature rather than the Creator....' (See Romans 1:25.) Satan's lie which suggests you can be *like* God, that you can possess the sovereign authority which in reality belongs only to God, motivates and controls much of our civilisation today. Man is trying to pull himself up by his own bootstraps; he is working to build his own utopia on earth and then, if he can, take it to outer space with him. Through some forms of psychological techniques; through world religions of various kinds (which deny the uniqueness of God's self–revelation in Jesus Christ, and deny the necessity of his saving work on the cross); through 'deification' of the earth itself, and in the worship of other 'gods', men are defying God and *deifying* themselves —they are playing right into the hands of Satan.

How did Eve respond to Satan's approach? She responded by making three mistakes. Firstly, she took away from the word of God. In Genesis 3:2, Eve omits the word 'freely'. Remember God had actually said, "Of every tree of the garden you may freely eat." (See 2:16.) It sounds as though Eve caught hold of Satan's ploy. When you start to question or forget the amazing grace and goodness of God, it starts to become much easier to disobey his will. Secondly, she added something to the word of God. We do not find the words 'nor shall you touch it' in God's original command; they are certainly not recorded. Not only did Eve make God's word seem less gracious by omitting the word 'freely', but she also made it sound harsh. She also altered God's word. God had not said 'lest you die'; what he had said was, "...for in the day that you eat of it you shall surely die" (2:17b).

The enemy made the penalty for disobedience seem to Eve much less harsh. Once you have treated God's word in this way, you are wide open to the devil's final trick. He prepared her mind: he merely encouraged Eve to consider the tree apart from God's word. She came to see what had been forbidden as a 'good', something which would be fine to eat, desirable to make one wise, and conferring some quality of being 'like God'.

She had to make a choice. Was she to act in line with God's word or Satan's word? We know what happened: she rejected God, believed Satan whose attack on her mind and heart had been successful, and she sinned. Adam, for his part proved to be just as much a sinner, since he, too, was willing to break the divine command and succumb to temptation. You and I have suffered the consequences of this disobedience of our first ancestors ever since. God accomplishes his will on earth through truth. Satan accomplished his purpose in that matter through lies.

When we put our trust in the Lord Jesus Christ, we are not left alone; we have the Spirit of God to work in and through us in power and truth, to help give us a victorious life.

When we believe a lie, Satan goes to work in our lives, for he is a liar and the father of lies. Faith in God's truth leads to victory; faith in Satan's lies leads to defeat. Beware! The devil is accomplished as an advertiser! He always presents his lies as being truth. Remember, he did not approach Eve as himself —he came as a serpent. He is a deceiver! Moreover, the church must continue to beware of his malign, deceptive work, as Paul reminds us:

> For such are false prophets, deceitful workers, transforming themselves into apostles of Christ. And no wonder! For Satan himself transforms himself into an angel of light.
>
> *2 Corinthians 11:13 –14*

Satan is a counterfeit, an imitator and a liar, and many

people, sadly, believe his deceptions. Everybody in the world lives by faith of one sort or another. Even atheism is a kind of 'faith', of a wholly negative and foolish sort. The difference between the Christian and the unconverted person is not the presence of a faith (of some kind), but the *object* of faith. The unsaved person may be trusting in himself, or in other people, or in false deities or ideology. The Christian puts his trust in God who is revealed to us in Jesus Christ.

It is faith in God—to whom we come only through Jesus, true God and true man—that is the secret of living a victorious life. If you have any residual doubt as to whether God honours those who have faith in him, just read Hebrews, chapter eleven. Trust in the Lord Jesus; put your faith in him! He offers the only true way forward. He alone is the way, the life and the truth.

In the workplace we find all manner of temptation in many matters of honesty, morality and conscience, at individual, corporate and social levels. Perhaps the fastest growing temptation (only one of many, of course) is internet pornography. Email 'spam' offers easy access to so many of these sites, and, for whatever reason, Christian men seem to be able to justify visiting 'just to have a quick look to see what it is that we are up against!' And then they continue to justify the activity on the basis that it does not hurt anybody really! The devil will encourage you to believe this lie if you give him the opportunity. If you sense that you are becoming entrapped in any such deception, make it a priority to read and meditate on Psalm 139. God does see, and he knows exactly what you are doing. If you doubt that he really requires of you inward purity of heart and will, think about Matthew 5:28,

"But I say to you that whoever looks at a woman to lust for her has already committed adultery with her in his heart."

Once the devil sees that you now have such a weakness, you are into a very serious spiritual battle. Claim the promise of 1 Corinthians 10:13 —

> No temptation has overtaken you except such as is common to man; but God is faithful, who will not allow you to be tempted beyond what you are able, but with the temptation will also make the way of escape, that you may be able to bear it.

Yes, God does allow us to be tempted, but he also, in his grace gives us a way out, and, 'If we confess our sins, He is faithful and just to forgive us our sins and to cleanse us from all unrighteousness' (1 John 1:9).

God is fully aware of our weaknesses, for he knows us better than we know ourselves. He always deals with us in his mercy and grace, providing a way out of all temptation.

Something is required of us: as we have already seen, when we are being tempted we must resist the devil, then, as the word promises, he will certainly flee; but if we have succumbed to temptation we must repent at once and ask God to forgive us. He will welcome us back with arms of love.

One of the reasons for the high rate of failure amongst Christian men is the fact that there are so many who are living in a spiritual infancy —finding any excuse not to grow on in to spiritual maturity. Many claim to know Christ as Saviour, but have no idea what it is that he can do for us as our wonderful high priest, Saviour and Lord. Many have been saved long enough for them to be teaching others, yet they have remained in, or lapsed into, 'spiritual childhood'. So sometimes it is necessary to be taught again and again, until we remember the things that we have forgotten. The recipients of the letter to the Hebrews were inexperienced in the word, yet what blessing there is for us when we hear again one of the great messages of that wonderful letter: about the word of God working with the Spirit of God, and our communication with God in prayer. Our relationship to the word of God determines our spiritual maturity. Experience and age do not count; we learn from God by reading his word and by prayer—the Spirit of the risen Christ

witnessing to our spirit. Nothing else will work.
Remember, those waning Hebrews had:

Drifted form the word;
Doubted the word; and had become
Dull to the word.

They had not mixed the word with faith nor sought to
practise it in their daily life. They had not exercised their
spiritual faculties, and therefore were growing dull and
ineffective. Instead of going forward in blessing and grace,
they were drifting backwards and away. Growing in grace
includes growing in knowledge. The more we know about
ourselves and about our Lord Jesus Christ the better we are
able to move forward and face life with absolute confidence.
We began this chapter by thinking of those things we need
to know about the one who is God's enemy and ours. The
works of Satan are more than unpleasant, and Christians find
it heavy and distasteful even to think of the foul works of
malice, hatred, deception and cruelty which mark the
tempter. In the Scriptures we are told as much as we need
to know about the opposition we face, so that we can reach
for the spiritual weapons we have at our disposal. This is a
very real battlefield, and God does not want his army to be
ill-equipped for their task.
So put on the armour and resist the assaults of the evil
one; be aware that he can attack anywhere on any day: at
home, in your workplace or indeed anywhere you find
yourself. Remember the power of the word of God—learnt,
absorbed and deployed under the anointing of the Holy Spirit;
and remember, above all, the power of the blood of
Jesus. Apply that precious blood. Claim its protection over
yourself, those you love, those with whom you work and the
tasks God has given you to do in his kingdom.

8

PERSECUTION, OPPOSITION AND PEACE

Let us note something significant about being a Christian in Western culture: we are not living under *direct* pressure to reject Christ, by which I mean institutional pressure from state authorities or other powerful established forces. In fact, in our society, having a little religion is still regarded by many as socially acceptable. Being a Christian *per se* does not keep us out of 'the system'. We can still enjoy having jobs. No one is pouring out death threats against us for attending church. We are not locked out of our society. In fact, it is probably widely regarded as all right to be a 'little bit Christian'. However, when we grow in the love and knowledge of our Lord Jesus Christ and change how we think, behave and respond, and as we grow more in conformity to the way God would have us be, then we can become a problem for those around us. We may begin to experience more subtle forms of abuse—ridicule, slander, exclusion and so on—for truly living out our faith. We may not be excluded from our communities, families or marriages (though such things are not unheard of), but certainly, we will sense the discomfort of being excluded in many other ways. This can be triggered when you have to take a stand for what you know to be right; maybe you refuse a graphology test; people begin to notice you do not talk with them about 'star signs', nor will you participate in inappropriate 'bonding' or 'focussing' or meditation techniques at those management or sales seminars. There are increasingly so many areas in which 'new age' thinking permeate corporate life and methods. Perhaps, working as a scientist in a science community, you have been dismissed as stupid by your peers for holding to a biblical creationist view, so you know in that way what it feels like to be excluded professionally.

If your former friends change their vocabulary and the tone of their discussion when you walk into the room, then you know what it feels like to be excluded. Perhaps you are misunderstood and emotionally mistreated by your unbelieving husband or wife —then you know in a very personal way what it feels like to be excluded. Maybe you are irritated over the derisive comments your parents or other members of your family make about your conversion to Christ, so you know what it feels like to be excluded in that way. If you feel misunderstood by your non-believing employer or colleagues for your honesty, integrity and unwillingness to cut corners in order to secure contracts, then you know what exclusion means.

If you are living through, or have lived through any one of these circumstances, you know the pain and anxiety that come with them. However, there is hope and encouragement for you. A positive present and an unimaginable and sensational future await you. The good news is that you are NOT excluded by God.

To see how this can be so, we will draw some key lessons from Peter's first letter. We begin with a brief look at Peter the man. There are a few things we need to recall about him. He announces that he is an apostle and the author of this brief but truly profound letter— 'Peter, an apostle of Jesus Christ...' (1:1). When he first met Jesus, his name had been Simon. He had been a fisherman and had grown up, lived and worked along the north–west corner of the Sea of Galilee. (See John 1:44.) Early in Jesus' public ministry, he called Simon to be one of his disciples. (See Mark 1:16 –18). It was Jesus who gave this fisherman his new name, Peter, meaning 'rock'. Peter was a *transformed individual*. Transforming Simon into 'Peter' was a large undertaking. We know that he had been an impatient and impulsive man, who often acted without thinking. Recall again that incident when a storm had blown up and they saw Jesus walking towards them on the water: almost instinctively, Peter stepped out of the boat and began walking to meet Jesus. That was a great, wholly good impulse of faith, of course; and walking towards Jesus is always an excellent impulse! Peter's other, less positive kind of impulsiveness was revealed on occasions when he spoke without thinking. When Jesus predicted his own arrest, death and the scattering of his followers, Peter dramatically and boastfully pledged his steadfast support against all odds—"Even if all are made to stumble, yet I will not be" (Mark 14:29b). Later that evening, Jesus was betrayed and arrested. A rooster crowed and this disciple adamantly denied his association with Jesus —three times! Simon Peter, far from standing up for Jesus, gave in to fear. Yet amazingly, and here is hope for all Christians, despite his weaknesses and faults, God chose Peter to be the recognized leader of the church. He did have some great moments, of course. He made the confession about Jesus that we must all make today—"You are the Christ, the Son of the living God" (Matthew 16:16b). After his denial, and following Jesus' resurrection, Peter was reconciled with his Lord. Above all, In Acts 2, we read the sermon that Peter preached after the coming of the Holy Spirit at Pentecost.

He became a faithful and fearless messenger. When this disciple identifies himself as an 'apostle of Jesus Christ', his letter is not to be seen as the pious opinions of a well-wishing friend, but as the authoritative word of one who speaks for the Lord of the church himself.

So what was Peter's message? Remember that the first century church to which Peter wrote was set in the Roman empire in the time of Nero, an evil man. Later in his reign he would order a bloodbath of persecution, which was to fall upon the Christian community. At this point, when Peter wrote his first epistle, the early signs of the persecution by Nero were already being experienced, mainly through slander, malicious gossip, misrepresentation, unemployment and exclusion from significant parts of the economic system. The Christians were suffering in many ways. So it was that Peter wrote: '...you have been grieved by various trials.'

They were suffering from an identity crisis. They had once belonged in—and actively participated in—their respective communities. However, the day these new converts confessed **Jesus is the Christ, the Son of the living God,** their lives were transformed in every way. Their friends did not know how to respond to them. Pagan husbands felt betrayed by their converted wives. Governing officials and employers became insecure, as converts to Christ changed their loyalties and allegiances. So these new Christians were left out—'strangers', struggling to live in their new identity. So Peter's task was huge —to encourage these 'scattered strangers' with the truth that they belonged to God. This apostle, who struggled with his own acceptance in the courtyard the night he denied Jesus, assured these new converts that while they may feel left out of this world indefinitely, they were assuredly adopted by God. In other words, while everyone else around you may be rejecting you, God—the Creator of the universe—has specifically and collectively chosen believers, including you, to be his own:

> ...a royal priesthood, a holy nation, His own special people....
>
> *See 1 Peter 2:9*

They were working together in a new community. During those difficult times that the Christians faced, what was the purpose of their suffering? The answer is initially given in chapter one, verse two — chosen as a new community, these early Christians were to, 'declare the praises of God' to other peoples, communities and nations. This has always been God's expectation of his people. Yes, they may be scattered about like seed, but God will use them to sow and reap a harvest for him —to his glory, and to their benefit. Peter does not want them to act disrespectfully, nor angrily, towards those outside their new community. Instead, they are to pray for and submit to those in authority over them. If they suffer as a result of doing good, they should interpret such mistreatment as an emblem of honour. After all, they are God's peculiar people, and they are to live for and obey the Lord Jesus, who went all the way to the cross for them. Consequently, these young believers are to walk individually and collectively in the steps of Jesus Christ—always a dangerous path, *but with delightful results*.

So we know a little about Peter and his message to the churches in Asia Minor. What relevance is there in this for us —today? It might be asked: what did Peter know about life in the twenty first century, with the fast-paced, industrialised, high-tech lifestyle which we experience? Well, I think that if Peter were on earth today he would tell us that life is life and people are people in every age, for the Bible addresses men and women as they really are at all times and in all places. Moreover, every Christian in every generation in every society, at every moment of history, has had to contend with the disturbing reality of resisting (and falling prey to) the distractions which come from other people and the deceptions of Satan during the journey through this alien world. There is no escaping this world. You have to pass through it to get home to heaven! Peter knew this very well, and his teaching and the account of his own life can bring us comfort, reassurance and the realization that we are not the first to undergo opposition and attacks, as well as having to have our own weaknesses ministered to.

As Christians, when we are suffering exclusion, we need, and can receive, a tremendously abundant outpouring of God's grace. When you look deeply into the life of Simon Peter, you find that he had been, as we observed, a truly flawed character. He knew only too well how he had let Jesus down at one stage, but after an amazing outpouring of the Holy Spirit, we can see very clearly indeed that his focus was outgoing, positive, full of assurance of the presence and power of the Lord. Read again that amazing sermon Peter preached at Pentecost! If one who had fallen so far as to deny Jesus could preach so powerfully under the power of God, you can see that with God nothing is impossible. No disciple need ever feel that they have been 'written off' as an irredeemable failure. And what letters Peter wrote! His first epistle is full of encouragement to believers to know and stand on the position they have been given by grace alone. No amount of opposition and social exclusion will deter a Christian in any age who has that wonderful assurance. Peter shows us that we need to be learning and resting on God's promises as to our standing as 'living stones' in the body of Christ.

Peter had needed correction from the Lord; he had needed forgiveness and restoration when he sinned. But what a wonderful transformation took place. What a source of peace it is for each of us —the knowledge that Jesus cares for each disciple so much that he does repair the damage we do; he really does love us so much that he gives us fresh opportunities, no matter how badly we have messed things up. When Jesus chose his original disciples, he picked the likes of Simon Peter. God continues to touch the hearts of people like you and me who, like Peter, have our flaws. We have our moments of living in the glorious awareness of the light of eternity. We also have our profoundly regretted moments of behaving badly in the dark cesspools of this world. Through both seasons of success and failure, it is the touch of God— undeserved grace from him— that keeps us focussed on who we are and what we are on earth to do: we are his own 'special people' who are to declare the praises of God, who called us out of darkness into his marvellous light, and we are to walk in obedience to Jesus, and in openness to the Holy Spirit.

In order to fulfil this divinely given purpose, we must reach out daily for the life–giving and life–sustaining grace that only God can give. Without it, we can wallow in the self–pity that so often follows personal failure or experience of opposition, or retreat to the familiarity of our former relationships and the host of worldly temptations that serve to divert us. Grace is God's way of keeping you where you really want and need to be!

When you face moments of failure and personal disappointment, the message of Peter would be: trust the wonderful grace of Jesus, our Lord and ever–loving Saviour. He will pick you up. Remember how Jesus restored Peter. He repeatedly asked Peter whether he loved him. He wanted Peter to affirm that, and re-affirm it, and keep re-affirming it. Think of those praise songs in which you sing repeatedly that you love Jesus; begin to sing such a song in your heart, over and over again. It is biblical! Do what Jesus told Peter to do and keep affirming your love for your Lord verbally. If you find that hard to do, then ask the Holy Spirit to fill you afresh until you can do it and mean it in your heart. When you stumble or fall, simply relax and let Jesus Christ pick you up with his life-giving grace and mercy. If you deny him with your life or words, then repent and let him fill your heart with love for him again. Whatever happens, do not give up! It is better to be a disciple of Jesus who fails and is restored than to be one who fails to hear the call and follow.

We need God's peace. When we are experiencing various kinds of 'social exclusion' which, as we have noted, can occur in our lives at work, home and in the community, as a direct or indirect result of our walking in faith and witnessing, we need to remember another message of 1 Peter: that God's peace is given and received even in the midst of suffering. True peace does not mean being exempt from suffering! Peter's readers were very well aware of that; Peter himself certainly knew it; we need to know it. **All too often, our idea of peace is worldly rather than scriptural.** We tend to think of peace as being the opposite of pain, and pain can be felt on various levels. If I feel the initial pains of a toothache, I start to panic, as I think about the possibilities of drillings and fillings. Even the anticipation of a little physical discomfort can have quite an impact on my thinking! At another level, to be mistreated by those who used to be your friends and loved ones can cause immense pain. In a Christian, pain can be felt when we hear our Lord's name taken in vain. There is the pain that accompanies the outworking of compassionate Christian love as you minister to the suffering. We would have to be insensible, insensitive, not to be aware of pain of many kinds in humanity all around us, as well as that which we experience ourselves. But the message of Peter's first epistle, which is the message of the New Testament as a whole, is that we *can* have peace, and lots of it, **regardless of the circumstances**. The peace that passes all understanding is a precious gift of God which is unaffected by all kinds of interior and external pain. No matter how persecuted you may be or feel, you can still be filled in a most amazing way with a wonderful peace, which flows directly from a right relationship with your heavenly Father.

We have to live in this world. We inevitably come up against many things which are abhorrent to us in the culture of our society at large as well as in whatever workplace culture we find ourselves; and we need much wisdom from above to show us when and how to react, when to be silent, and when to withdraw from what others are doing and saying around us. At a very mundane level, there are times when we cannot watch some programmes on the television as their content is so offensive to all that we believe and stand for. But we can have peace and know that we have other alternatives. We may have to deny ourselves certain films or books, but we can have peace, knowing that God is pleased and glorified because of our choices. We may be resisting the temptation to plot against someone who has hurt us, but we can leave such hurts at the foot of the cross, release forgiveness and know that God is both just and merciful, and experience his abundant peace. With wisdom from above there is always another, better way than the way of conformity to the world's evil.

In this matter of peace, it is also worth mentioning in passing that you can have peace as you stand your ground in the science debates (creationism v. evolution; Does science contradict faith? —and so on) in the knowledge that God will sustain you with *his* peace as you do so. That sort of issue has become far easier to handle now that old–fashioned 'mechanistic' theories of the nature of the world and the universe have been largely supplanted by more open–ended cosmologies, and as it has become better known among the public that a fair number of scientists are also Christians. But make sure, again, that you exercise wisdom and discernment as to when and how to engage in such issues. You cannot argue someone to the cross, and whilst an intelligent colleague or friend might be sufficiently convinced by your reasoning to accept that it is not irrational to believe that God exists, it remains as true as ever that faith in Jesus Christ crucified, our only Lord and Saviour, seems like 'foolishness' to the worldly, until they have had a personal encounter with him. The revelation that the Christian claims about Jesus — that he is the Way, the Truth and the Life, and that no-one comes to the Father except through him, and that this is universally true in all times and places—are so contrary to the world view of our contemporaries as to be a massive shock to them!

In all the ways in which the world would try to get you to conform—in your thinking, behaviour and speech—you can and must say 'no' to those who put you under pressure, knowing that your heavenly Father loves you and will give you *his* peace. Compromise with the world does not bring peace. Always be ready to take a stand for honesty and integrity in the workplace, knowing that God's peace will sustain you. You may feel left out of this world, but to be in line with God's will is essential for true peace.

Quite simply, the message that Peter wrote to those churches nearly two thousand years ago is as important and relevant today as it was then. Throughout Christian history, believers have endured mistreatment on account of Jesus Christ. Sometimes their stand has cost them their lives (and continues to do so in some parts of the world). As we have noted, suffering also came in the form of ridicule, slander, social exclusion and unemployment. Peter understood the conflict with the world that Christians face. He wrote to encourage them, and to point to the sustaining grace of God: sustaining Christians until the work of salvation is complete; sustaining them in their submission to earthly authorities; sustaining them through their personal suffering. The same is true for you and me; now, as then. Honestly, we may be left out of our families, relationships, neighbourhoods, peer groups and workplace networks for clinging to the sustaining grace of God. But whenever we are left out of this world, we must remember that our strength comes from an eternal relationship with God, who chose us, redeemed us and is perfecting us, creating in us the very image of his Son, Jesus, through the Spirit, who indwells us and is sanctifying us.

Hold on to these precious truths —all through your working day, at home, office or even during family and leisure times; remember your special calling, God's infinite personal love for you, your fellowship with him, his mighty promises, and his perfect parenting of you, his adopted child. No-one and nothing, no circumstances however bleak, neither persecution nor opposition, can destroy what God has done for you, or your special place in his perfect heart of love. Return again and again to that first letter of Peter until you know this in your heart as well as your mind, and you will be full of God's peace.

9

LIVING HOPE

Is there any hope for an individual who always has his 'foot in his mouth', or one who 'blows hot and cold', or one who can say things that bring high praise one moment and things which earn a severe rebuke the next? Is there any hope for those of us who make many mistakes, topple into pitfalls and are slow to learn?

The answer is definitely in the affirmative, for Christians have been given an amazing hope. We are always to be full of hope concerning all that God can do —both in our own lives and the lives of others. With him, as Jesus assured us, nothing is impossible.

'Hope', of one kind or another, or a search for hope, seems to be an almost ineradicable feature of human life 'in the natural'. Only in the most extreme and dire circumstances does it seem to disappear altogether, to be replaced by depression and despair. It is indeed necessary for human health and well–being. Admittedly, people are looking for the fulfilment of their hopes in a lot of wrong places. Have you tried to pay for petrol at your local garage an hour before the lottery draw? So often there are tens of people, lined up in front of the counter, paying for their lottery tickets, hoping to win millions. Some time ago, I was speaking at a residential conference, and there was a sign over the reception that said, *When my ship comes in, I'll probably be on a train somewhere!* What a tragic mixture of spurious, worldly false 'hope' and tragic resignation that sentiment represented! The truth is that there is a true, living hope which is offered to everybody, but it is yet another aspect of man's fallenness that the searching and seeking is so often for the wrong sorts of fulfilment —fulfilment of distorted, unworthy or secondary objects of hope, rather than for the one real source of a true and living hope.

What Christians have been given—to enjoy, and to proclaim to others—is a living hope; a life–giving hope; a hope that is sure and steadfast; a hope which is grounded in a living relationship with God. Our hope is set in him, and in his sure promises which will certainly be fulfilled. As Paul puts it:

> For I consider that the sufferings of this present time are not worthy to be compared with the glory which shall be revealed in us.
>
> *Romans 8:18*

LIVING HOPE CHANGES YOUR LIFE

We may say that we are Bible–believing Christians, but all too often when we examine ourselves carefully, as we should, we see that our hopes are centred on the wrong objects. The ever–present temptation is to place our hope in ourselves, our friends, our family and our material circumstances. We may be placing our hope in our jobs or our prospects for advancement; we may sometimes repose a good deal of hope in what our doctors can do. Some of these hopes, under God, have a limited, secondary place, but none of them is the ground of the real *living hope*.

The hope of the Christian is rooted in the God and Father of Jesus Christ, and he can never fail. Why? Because his word is true; his promises are sure; his salvation is eternal.

LIVING HOPE ISSUES FROM AN ABUNDANT MERCY

Our sin is, and always was, an offence to God. He could have cast us off forever. But in his great mercy, because he loved us, he sent his Son Jesus into this world to become a human being like us — *unlike* us, to live a sinless life, to give that sinless life as a propitiation, so that we who are guilty and should be punished by death might be declared innocent because we have been forgiven by the very one we offended. Just think about it: Jesus took our sin upon himself and now, since we received him, God treats us as if we had never sinned at all. What mercy!

LIVING HOPE AND THE NEW BIRTH

At our first birth we were born sinners because of the sins of Adam; by our first birth we grew up to be enemies of God; by our first birth we could never please God, no matter how hard we tried. Nonetheless, God caused us to be born again by grace, through faith in Jesus Christ. Our new birth adopts us into the family of God, brings us a brand new life, and enables us to please God and live for him, worship him, and become more like him as he restores his image in us, and to go at last to live with him forever. What we need to know at a very deep level is that when we were born again it was, above all, **new birth to a living hope**. This is made clear by Peter, when he writes:

> Blessed be the God and Father of our Lord Jesus Christ, who according to His abundant mercy has begotten us again to a living hope through the resurrection of Jesus Christ from the dead.
>
> *1 Peter 1:3*

Our living experience of the reality of the new birth places in our hearts the reality of the hope for eternity. As God's new creatures, we have already begun to experience many good things; eternal life has already begun for us; and a true hope for the best things yet to come is firmly in our spirit. We do not need false hopes of lottery wins because our treasure is already in heaven. The lottery winners will one day, sooner or later, make the sad discovery that their winnings are for this world only.

LIVING HOPE IS MADE CERTAIN BY THE RESURRECTION OF JESUS CHRIST FROM THE DEAD

After his crucifixion, Jesus did not remain dead. He died for us, but the Father raised him from the dead. His resurrection proved beyond all doubt that his sacrifice was accepted by the Father. His resurrection assures us that our sins are really forgiven by the one who has defeated the enemy. His resurrection proved that he is able to give us this new life too; that we are raised from the death of sin into the glory of the new life, that he is able to keep us forever and that he is able to take us to heaven when we die. 'The last enemy to be destroyed is death.' How hollow all worldly hopes look in the light of the reality of death for the whole human race. But Jesus truly has overcome sin and death, and we who have received him as our Lord and Saviour will enjoy the fruit of that amazing victory. Many reliable witnesses saw the risen Jesus. The evidence is firm and sure. This foundational truth of the Christian faith does not depend, as so many religions and philosophies do, upon human theories, ideologies, philosophy or speculation: there is, at the heart of Christianity the testimony of many, many witnesses. The testimony is recorded in the New Testament, and if that testimony had been untrue then it would very quickly have been exposed and faith in the risen Lord Jesus would have died out. But the testimony was true, and it accords with all the prophetic witness and preparation that we read in the

Old Testament. Yes, our living hope comes from the living God, and he determined that human witnesses would see the risen Lord Jesus Christ, and testify to what they had seen for themselves. What a wonderful, true hope we have been given; and how amazing that God has enabled us to have the certitude that comes not only from our own spiritual experience but also from witnesses whose words are recorded for us and for all generations. The Christian faith is unique; the testimony to the resurrection is unique; our Christian living hope of our own resurrection to be with our Lord is unique. Our Lord's claim to be *the* Way, *the* Truth and *the* Life is confirmed and sealed for ever.

This is the living hope that will keep us going through every trial. For there are trials on the way. This life, since the Fall, has never been easy, nor free of difficulty, sorrow and suffering. Too many people base their whole lives on the false idea that life should be easy. That there is a supposed 'right' to the 'pursuit of happiness' in and of itself is not a biblical notion. Rather, we pursue God, and a closer walk of obedience to him. Even Christians get seduced by false philosophy at times, and wonder why they have to go through any trials. We, too, have struggles; we, too, have financial collapses; we, too, have people break their promises or act terribly toward us; we, too, get concerned about our children; we, too, face health problems. We, too, face death; there are no exemptions just because you are a Christian. But for us death is not a tragedy, nor do we face it with uncertainty, perplexity or despair. A believer dies full of a living hope, which will be fulfilled. There need be no fear of judgement when you know as personal Saviour the only one who could deal with sin. Deep down, you know that, don't you? On your journey through life thus far you may perhaps already have been to a few places that you should not have visited, and probably have had more than a few problems. But the living hope that Jesus gives will keep you and sustain you until the moment when you meet him face to face.

I remember well one Saturday morning when my father took me with him to see a friend of his, who was a jeweller. We went down a little back road, off North Street in Leeds. To be honest, it was a murky place; when we entered that Dickensian building it was like stepping back two hundred years. In the corner of the workshop there was a small furnace which was burning something almost white hot. The jeweller told me that he was separating some gold and platinum. They had been mixed together, and even the gold was of two different kinds. I asked how hot it was. His answer was, 'very hot indeed!' Then I watched as he poured the precious metals out, deftly separating the contents into three different small flasks. After that, he poured chemicals over them, which made a most awful smell. Then he reheated the metals—separately this time—then poured on more chemicals. He was hoping that, by the end of the day, he would have some eighteen carat gold, some twenty four carat gold and pure platinum, but he would not know if he could re-use the metals until they had been taken to an assay office for testing! Here is the answer for all Christians:

> ...that the genuineness of your faith, being much more precious than gold that perishes, though it is tested by fire, may be found to praise, honor, and glory at the revelation of Jesus Christ....
>
> *1 Peter 1:7*

This is what God is in the process of doing with you and me. As you face all those trials and tests that seem so difficult; as you encounter opposition to your faith and the stand you have to take; and whichever of the various forms of exclusion which we discussed earlier in this book apply to you —all these things are used by him, as he separates you for his service and makes you holy.

> And we know that all things work together for good to those who love God, to those who are called according to His purpose.
>
> *Romans 8:28*

'All things' means all things. Even things which seem to be contrary to the will of God are encompassed by that term 'all things'. So there is never any reason to fret, fuss or despair. God has his hand on every part of your life. He is continuing to do that work in you which began when you first came to Christ. But if all that your trials do is make you angry, resentful or bitter, then you are refusing to allow God to fulfil his best purpose for you in this life.

God requires that, in the here and now, you should show forth his grace in your personality, reflecting his glory in this present world, so that others may look at you and learn the value of the faith which you claim.

When we get irritable, unreasonable and bad-tempered, we spoil something in the good work that God is doing in us, which is designed to show through us that this faith which we seek to demonstrate before the world really does make a difference; we risk bringing the name of God into disrepute if we grumble or become discontented.

LIVING HOPE IS CENTRED IN JESUS CHRIST OUR SAVIOUR

We have not seen our Saviour with our physical eyes but have seen him with spiritual eyes of faith. We shall see our Lord face to face one day. But having not seen him, yet we love him. There is the great, overarching reality about the Christian life. What does it mean to be a Christian? It means to love our Lord Jesus; to love God with all our heart, mind, soul and strength. It is to love him in spite of the fact that we have not seen him with our eyes.

Down deep inside our hearts is a joy that cannot be explained, stopped or, for that matter, controlled. It is a joy that is not natural but supernatural in origin; it is a joy that is not just emotional, though why should we expect the emotions to be unaffected? It is a joy that is rooted in your relationship with God, and there is nothing that can destroy that which God has placed in our hearts. This joy arises out of the certain knowledge that God is in overall control of our lives, even whilst we are in the process of being refined for his service and prepared for heaven.

WITNESS AND WORK

When we talk about witnessing to the truth of the good news, we must remember always that the words of our mouths are ineffective if their truth is not also seen in our daily walk of faith.

The truth is simply this: we should be the most contented and most joyous people who journey through this world which is trying so very hard to make us conform to its corrupt standards. This joy should shine out through every aspect and attitude of our lives. I do not mean that we should walk around with a silly grin on our faces all the time. But everything about us should speak to others of our relationship to the God who has saved us from his own wrath and from hell, through the saving death and glorious resurrection of his own dear Son.

God loves you with an everlasting and absolutely perfect love, and that should put a genuine smile on your face, gladness in your heart, true light in your life and a bounce in your steps: at work, at home and indeed everywhere you find yourself at each moment —and all this speaks about him, for inside you the power that raised Jesus from the dead is at work, the power of the new creation. What an awesome truth! To God be all the praise and glory.

When your words and your life match... then witnessing is just being you —*you, in Christ!*